Also by Myra Cohn Livingston

Come Away
   (*A Margaret K. McElderry Book*)
Happy Birthday!
I'm Hiding
The Malibu: and Other Poems
   (*A Margaret K. McElderry Book*)
The Moon and a Star: and Other Poems
The Way Things Are: and Other Poems
   (*A Margaret K. McElderry Book*)
When You Are Alone/It Keeps You Capone:
   An Approach to Creative Writing with Children
   (*A Margaret K. McElderry Book*)
Wide Awake: and Other Poems
4-Way Stop: and Other Poems
   (*A Margaret K. McElderry Book*)

Edited by Myra Cohn Livingston

Listen, Children, Listen: Poems for the Very Young
The Poems of Lewis Carroll
Speak Roughly to Your Little Boy: A Collection of
   Parodies and Burlesques, Together with the Original
   Poems, Chosen and Annotated for Young People
A Tune Beyond Us: A Collection of Poems
What a Wonderful Bird the Frog Are: An Assortment
   of Humorous Poetry and Verse
One Little Room, An Everywhere: Poems of Love
   (*A Margaret K. McElderry Book*)
O Frabjous Day: Poetry for Holidays and
   Special Occasions
   (*A Margaret K. McElderry Book*)

O FRABJOUS DAY!

O FRABJOUS DAY!

POETRY FOR HOLIDAYS
AND SPECIAL OCCASIONS

EDITED BY

MYRA COHN LIVINGSTON

A Margaret K. McElderry Book

ATHENEUM 1977 NEW YORK

Library of Congress Cataloging in Publication Data

O frabjous day!
"A Margaret K. McElderry book."
Summary: More than 100 poems commemorating high days,
holidays, and days of sorrow, including Valentines' Day,
Halloween, Christmas, Chanukah, and the assassinations
of some famous Americans.
1. Holidays—Juvenile poetry. 2. American poetry.
[1. Holidays—Poetry. 2. American poetry—Collections]
I. Livingston, Myra Cohn.
PZ8.3.O18   811'.008   76-28510
ISBN 0-689-50076-9

Published simultaneously in Canada by
McClelland & Stewart, Ltd.
Manufactured in the United States of America
by The Book Press, Brattleboro, Vermont
Designed by Suzanne Haldane
First Edition

KN NOV '77

ACKNOWLEDGMENTS

The editor and publisher thank the following for permission to reprint the copyrighted material listed below:

ACUM LTD. for "Birth" by Amir Gilboa and "Piyyut for Rosh Hashana" by Chaim Guri.

ATHENEUM PUBLISHERS for "Thanksgiving" from *The Life Beside This One* by John N. Morris, copyright © 1975 by John N. Morris. "For the Coming Year" from *Collecting the Animals* by Peter Everwine, copyright © 1972 by Peter Everwine. "Twilight's Last Gleaming" by Arthur W. Monks from *Jiggery-Pokery* edited by Anthony Hecht and John Hollander, copyright © 1966 by Anthony Hecht and John Hollander. "Another Year Come" from *The Moving Target* by W. S. Merwin, copyright © 1960, 1963 by W. S. Merwin. (This poem originally appeared in *The New Yorker*.) "Conversation with Washington" and "Halloween" from *4-Way Stop and Other Poems* by Myra Cohn Livingston (A Margaret K. McElderry Book), copyright © 1976 by Myra Cohn Livingston.

GERALD W. BARRAX for "Christmas 1959 Et Cetera."

BEACON PRESS for "Death of Dr. King" #1 and #2 from *Generations* by Sam Cornish, copyright © 1968, 1969, 1970, 1971 by Sam Cornish.

BLACK SPARROW PRESS for "New Year's" by Charles Rezenikoff, copyright by Charles Reznikoff.

BROADSIDE PRESS for "Assassination" by Don L. Lee from *Don't Cry, Scream,* copyright © 1969 by Don L. Lee.

SIMON CAMPBELL for "I Will Go with My Father A-Ploughing" and "Harvest Song" by Joseph Campbell.

CHELSEA MAGAZINE for "The Light Year" by John Ridland, #34, October, 1975. Copyright © 1975 by John Ridland.

CONSTABLE PUBLISHERS for "Easter Sunday" translated by Helen Waddell in *Medieval Latin Lyrics* and "On the Birth of His Son" by Su Tung-Po translated by Arthur Waley from *170 Chinese Poems*.

CONTENTS

O FRABJOUS DAY!

By Way of an Introduction
(For L.A. and M.R.)

During his lifetime Lewis Carroll received any number of queries from puzzled readers who wished to have the meaning of words he used in his poems explained more fully. Time and again he would answer by writing back that he was "only talking nonsense."

Replying to a letter from the Lowrie children on April 6, 1876, he wrote:

> I'm very much afraid I didn't mean anything but non-sense! Still, you know, words mean more than we mean to express when we use them: so a good book ought to mean a great deal more than the writer meant. So, whatever good meanings are in the book, I'm very glad to accept as the meaning of the book.

It was undoubtedly a reading of "Jabberwocky" in *Through the Looking-Glass, and What Alice Found There* that prompted one of his child-friends, Maud Standen, to ask about words she found perplexing. Writing to her on December 18, 1877, Carroll answered:

> I am afraid I can't explain "vorpal blade" for you—nor yet "tulgey wood"; but I did make an explanation once for "uffish thought"—it seems to suggest a state of mind when the voice is gruffish, the manner roughish, and

the temper huffish. Then again, as to "burble": if you take the three verbs "*b*leat," "m*ur*mur" and "war*ble*," and select the bits I have underlined, it certainly *makes* "burble": though I am afraid I can't distinctly remember having made it that way.

Certainly the constant questions must have prompted him to include in the "Humpty Dumpty" chapter of *Through the Looking-Glass,* "Humpty-Dumpty's theory, of two meanings packed into one word like a portmanteau." In his introduction to *The Hunting of the Snark,* Carroll again gives his readers another clue:

For instance, take the two words, "fuming" and "furious." Make up your mind that you will say both words, but leave it unsettled which you will say first. Now open your mouth and speak. If your thoughts incline ever so little towards "fuming," you will say "fuming-furious;" if they turn, by even a hair's breadth, towards "furious," you will say "furious-fuming;" but if you have that rarest of gifts, a perfectly balanced mind, you will say "frumious."

As an admirer of Carroll and of his unsurpassed nonsense poem "Jabberwocky," I have chosen to call this anthology *O Frabjous Day,* in the hope that those who open this book will remember the sixth stanza of the poem:

"And, hast thou slain the Jabberwock?
    Come to my arms, my beamish boy!
O frabjous day! Callooh! Callay!"
    He chortled in his joy.

Somehow (and perhaps because of the word *joy* in the last line) I had always thought of the phrase "O frabjous day!" as an expression of great excitement and happiness. But the more poems I collected for this anthology, the more troubled I grew, for it became apparent to me that whereas holidays can be joyous, they can also be fraught with unhappiness, sad memories, or worry. Some people welcome the New Year, but in our uncertain world we may actually find it difficult to face. In the same way, our national heroes, Washington, Lincoln, or even Columbus, who discovered America, did not achieve through easy means. Easter may mean colored eggs and bunnies to some, but more importantly it recalls a religious sequence of the Crucifixion, Good Friday, and the Ascension. Many holidays are celebrated as a day away from school or work, but the underlying meaning ranges from grief for those who have died in war to those who have given their lives for freedom or civil rights or have died through assassination (and we've had our share of that in the world today). And so it goes with Halloween, Thanksgiving, or Christmas. We call each a holiday—but the poems I have chosen reveal more than just jolly jack-o'-lanterns, a plump stuffed turkey, or toys beneath a Christmas tree. The poems are written not necessarily about the actual event, but reflect the spirit behind the special day—and whereas many *are* joyful or abound in levity (which is tremendously important, for we all need to keep a sense of humor in our times), others may be more thought-provoking and reflect a more sobering attitude.

So I began to think about the portmanteau word

"frabjous" and discovered in the Oxford Dictionary that "frab" was in dialectic use about 1848; it means "harass" or "worry." Webster's Dictionary defines it as a verb, which means "to scold, worry, nag, to struggle or contend as in an argument." Webster also defines the word "frabjous" as an adjective—"A nonsense word with the general sense of 'surpassing' coined by Lewis Carroll (C. L. Dodgson)."

Putting all of this together (and sensing that the last part of the word—"jous"—must be a contraction of the word "joyous," because the boy is indeed filled with joy after slaying the Jabberwock), I have reached the conclusion that "frabjous" might indeed mean surpassing, in the sense that given a certain worry or harassment and being able to conquer it would produce a sense of well-being. But the word "surpassing" would also seem to carry the meaning of doing better than someone else, to go beyond, to be greater than—and I find this definition disturbing.

Perhaps "O frabjous day!" is instead a day that brings with it a mingling of worries and of joy—an occasion that stirs in the poet or the reader a regard for the tradition that has made it a day to remember, a touchstone by which men have marked and molded their lives and which they will continue to celebrate in their future.

It is entirely possible, however, that this is not the answer—that each reader will have to discover it for himself.

M. C. L.

To Celebrate

The New Year

. . . let the New Year in

FOR THE COMING YEAR

With the stars
rising again in my hands

Let my left arm be a rooster
it will keep the watches of the night

And let my right arm be an axe
it will be sleepless in the gate of morning

When I fold them to me
they will take things into their circle

They will sing softly to each other
softly

Peter Everwine (American, 1930–)

ANOTHER YEAR COME

I have nothing new to ask of you,
Future, heaven of the poor.
I am still wearing the same things.

I am still begging the same question
By the same light,
Eating the same stone,

And the hands of the clock still knock without entering.

W. S. Merwin (American, 1927–)

ON NEW YEAR'S EVE

Farther and farther from the three Pa Roads,
I have come three thousand miles, anxious and watchful,
Through pale snow-patches in the jagged night-moun-
    tains—
A stranger with a lonely lantern shaken in the wind.
. . . Separation from my kin
Binds me closer to my servants—
Yet how I dread, so far adrift,
New Year's Day, tomorrow morning!

Ts'uei T'u (Chinese, Ninth Century)
TRANSLATED BY WITTER BYNNER

THE LIGHT YEAR

it starts out
a small rod
the size of a pocket
flashlight
instantaneously
it accelerates
to one hundred
per cent of itself
and begins to travel

in eight minutes it
has passed our sun
on its new year's day

now August
the little tube
or rod is still travelling
through the dark of space
a tunnel
going through itself

summer ends   Halloween
approaches   Thanksgiving
Christmas rises
the little rod
never doubting
drives right on
it thinks it can

and it does   it reaches
new year's eve

no place to celebrate
far from home
and still so far
from any neighboring star
in the spacious
dark

John Ridland (*American, 1933–*)

NEW YEAR'S WATER

Here we bring new water from the well so clear,
For to worship God with, this happy New Year.
Sing levy dew, sing levy dew, the water and the wine,
With seven bright gold wires, and bugles that do shine.
Sing reign of fair maid, with gold upon her toe,
Open you the west door, and turn the Old Year go.
Sing reign of fair maid, with gold upon her chin,
Open you the east door, and let the New Year in.

Anonymous
TRADITIONAL WELSH

From: ORAGA HARU

For a fresh start
At the New Year
I named the old Yatarō
"A cup of tea."

(I have no servant to draw the first water of the New
   Year:)

But look! A crow comes
In his stead
To bathe in the water
On New Year's Day.

Child as he is
He bows his head
To the sacred offerings
Of the New Year.

Issa (Japanese, 1763–1827)
TRANSLATED BY NOBUYUKI YUASA

Both my child
And the New Year
Stood on their feet
This very morning.

Teitoku (Japanese, 1571–1653)
TRANSLATED BY NOBUYUKI YUASA

SPRING THOUGHTS

Finch-notes and swallow-notes tell the new year . . .
But so far are the Town of the Horse and the Dragon
    Mound
From this our house, from these walls and Han Gardens,
That the moon takes my heart to the Tartar sky.
I have woven in the frame endless words of my grieving

   . . .
Yet this petal-bough is smiling now on my lonely sleep.
. . . Oh, ask General Tou when his flags will come
    home
And his triumph will be carved on the rock of Yen-jan
    Mountain!

Huang-fu Jan (Chinese, Eighth Century)
TRANSLATED BY WITTER BYNNER

RESOLUTION

The ground is white with snow.
It's morning, of New Year's Eve, 1968, & clean
City air is alive with snow, it's quiet
Driving. I am 33. Good Wishes, brothers, everywhere

& Don't You Tread On Me.

Ted Berrigan (American, 1934–   )

NEW YEAR'S SONG

Now there comes
 The Christmas rose
 But that is eerie
    too like a ghost
 Too like a creature
     preserved under glass
 A blind white fish
    from an underground lake
 Too like last year's widow
    at a window
     And the worst cold's to come.

Now there comes
 The tight-vest lamb
 With its wriggle-eel tail
     and its wintry eye
 With its ice-age mammoth
     unconcern
 Letting the aeon
    seconds go by
 With its little peg hooves
    to dot the snow
 Following its mother
    into worse cold and worse
     And the worst cold's to come.

Now there comes
    The weak-neck snowdrops
    Bouncing like fountains
         and they stop you, they make you
    Take a deep breath
         make your heart shake you
    Such a too much of a gift
          for such a mean time
    Nobody knows
        how to accept them
    All you can do
        is gaze at them baffled
          And the worst cold's to come.

And now there comes
    The crocus
    To be nibbled by the starving hares
          to be broken by snow
    Now comes the aconite
        purpled by cold
    Now comes a song
        into the storm-cock's fancy
    And the robin and the wren
        they rejoice like each other
    In an hour of sunlight
        for something important
         Though the worst cold's to come.

Ted Hughes (English, 1930–   )

RING OUT, WILD BELLS

(FROM: IN MEMORIAM, CVI)

Ring out, wild bells, to the wild sky,
   The flying clouds, the frosty light:
   The year is dying in the night;
Ring out, wild bells, and let him die.

Ring out the old, ring in the new,
   Ring happy bells, across the snow:
   The year is going, let him go;
Ring out the false, ring in the true.

Ring out the grief that saps the mind,
   For those that here we see no more;
   Ring out the feud of rich and poor,
Ring in redress for all mankind.

Ring out a slowly dying cause,
   And ancient forms of party strife;
   Ring in the nobler modes of life,
With sweeter manners, purer laws.

Ring out the want, the care, the sin,
   The faithless coldness of the times;
   Ring out, ring out thy mournful rhymes,
But ring the fuller minstrel in.

Ring out false pride in place and blood,
  The civic slander and the spite;
  Ring in the love of truth and right,
Ring in the common love of good.

Ring out old shapes of foul disease;
  Ring out the narrowing lust of gold;
  Ring out the thousand wars of old,
Ring in the thousand years of peace.

Ring in the valiant man and free,
  The larger heart, the kindlier hand;
  Ring out the darkness of the land,
Ring in the Christ that is to be.

Alfred, Lord Tennyson (English, 1809–1892)

Birth, Birthdays, and Christenings

Make good thoughts . . .

SATURDAY'S CHILD

Some are teethed on a silver spoon,
    With the stars strung for a rattle;
I cut my teeth as the black raccoon—
    For implements of battle.

Some are swaddled in silk and down,
    And heralded by a star;
They swathed my limbs in a sackcloth gown
    On a night that was black as tar.

For some, godfather goddame
    The opulent fairies be;
Dame Poverty gave me my name,
    And Pain godfathered me.

For I was born on Saturday—
    "Bad time for planting a seed,"
Was all my father had to say,
    And, "One mouth more to feed."

Death cut the strings that gave me life,
  And handed me to Sorrow,
The only kind of middle wife
  My folks could beg or borrow.

Countee Cullen (American, 1903–1946)

MY STARS

On the day I was born,
The unalterable stars altered.
If I decided to sell lamps,
It wouldn't get dark till the day I died.

Some stars. Whatever I do
I'm a failure before I begin.
If I suddenly decided to sell shrouds,
People would suddenly stop dying.

Abraham Ibn Ezra (Spanish, 1089–1164)
TRANSLATED BY ROBERT MEZEY

CHRISTENING-DAY WISHES FOR MY GOD-CHILD GRACE LANE BERKLEY II

In Lieu of Silver Cup, Spoon, or Other Riches

Though no kin to those fine glistening
Dames at Sleeping Beauty's christening,
I wish such wishes as I may,
Juniper, on your Christening Day.

May you grow up strong and good
As old Maine wild-apple wood,
With a face that lights and shines
Like the west wind in white pines.
May your disposition be
Like the sun-glints on the sea,
Chickadees in snow or rain
Or the wild strawberries of Maine.
I wish that every sharp Maine thing—
Fringe of gentian, seagull's wing,
Seed of sweetfern, bayberry's rind—
Leave its marks upon your mind.
So you cannot, if you would,
Grow up anything but good.
And especially do take care
To grow into the name you bear:
Be green in Winter, love the ledge,
Be points of stars, the emerald's edge,

And though the world turn six and seven,
Bear the fruit that looks like heaven.
Grow up rainbows after rain,
Grow up, Juniper, like Maine!

Robert P. Tristam Coffin (American, 1892–1955)

PERAMBULATOR POEM

When I was christened
they held me up
and poured some water
out of a cup.

The trouble was
it fell on me,
and I and water
don't agree.

A lot of christeners
stood and listened:
I let them know
that I was christened.

David McCord (American, 1897–   )

BIRTH

The rain is over.

Yet from branches and eaves
It whispers in my ears
And covers my face
With a bluish bridal veil.

Good for you, God,
The child is caught in your net.
Now I shall bring leaf close to leaf,
Now I shall watch how leaf covers leaf
And the drops run together,
And I'll summon to my wedding
The swallows out of the sky,
And crown my window with flower pots.

Good for you, God.
The child is caught in your net.
I open my eyes—
My land is very wide,
Everything a field of tangled
Green buds.

O God, how embraced we have been!

Amir Gilboa (Israeli, 1917–)
TRANSLATED BY ROBERT MEZEY
AND SHULA STARKMAN

THE BIRTHPLACE

Here further up the mountain slope
Than there was ever any hope,
My father built, enclosed a spring,
Strung chains of wall round everything,
Subdued the growth of earth to grass,
And brought our various lives to pass.
A dozen girls and boys we were.
The mountain seemed to like the stir,
And made of us a little while—
With always something in her smile.
Today she wouldn't know our name.
 (No girl's, of course, has stayed the same.)
The mountain pushed us off her knees
And now her lap is full of trees.

Robert Frost *(American, 1874–1963)*

SONG FOR THE NEWBORN

Grande Pueblos
   To be sung by the one who first
   takes the child from its mother.

Newborn, on the naked sand
Nakedly lay it.
Next to the earth mother,
That it may know her;
Having good thoughts of her, the food giver.

Newborn, we tenderly
In our arms take it,
Make good thoughts.
House-god, be entreated,
That it may grow from childhood to manhood,
Happy, contented;
Beautifully walking
The trail to old age.
Having good thoughts of the earth its mother,
That she may give it the fruits of her being.
Newborn, on the naked sand
Nakedly lay it.

Mary Austin (American, 1868–1934)

ON THE BIRTH OF HIS SON

Families when a child is born
Hope it will turn out intelligent.
I, through intelligence
Having wrecked my whole life,
Only hope that the baby will prove
Ignorant and stupid.
Then he'll be happy all his days
And grow into a cabinet minister.

Su Tung-Po (Chinese, 1036–1101)
TRANSLATED BY ARTHUR WALEY

Crawl, laugh
Do as you wish—
For you are two years old
This morning.

Issa (Japanese, 1763–1827)
TRANSLATED BY NOBUYUKI YUASA

Birthday of but a single pang
That there are less to come—
Afflictive is the Adjective
But affluent the doom—

Emily Dickinson (American, 1830–1886)

TRALA TRALA TRALA LA-LE-LA

When the time has arrived
for your birthday
which I celebrate not with dancing
but a measured tread

we must join hands
what else can we do?
create a measure ignoring
what we had to do

when we were young at
a celebration—let's
eat our cake and have
it too dancingly

as we may flinging
our feet upward and out
to the end of time trala
trala trala la-le-la

William Carlos Williams
(American, 1883–1963)

BIRTHDAY GIFTS

"What will you have for your birthday?"
Said the woman heating her pan;
"A slim white swan, or a crimson rose,
A cat, or a little black man?

"What will you choose?" said the woman,
Stooping at the charcoal fire:
"A dappled foal, or a little white dog,
Or the largest horse in the shire?

"What will you have for your birthday?
Brown birds of lovely note,
Or a peacock with a hundred eyes
And no tune in his throat?

"What will you choose, pretty lady?
A county with its herds?
Or will you ride the summer sky
In a coach of ladybirds?"

"I do not choose a little white dog,"
Said Anne; "I want no herds:
Or a peacock with a hundred eyes,
Or a coach of ladybirds.

"I do not want a slim white swan,
Or a rose," said Lady Anne;
"But I will choose your charcoal fire,
Your ladle and rusted pan!"

She held her hand to the drifting smoke;
"I see what I desire!"
But the lady had floated into the leaves
With the blue mist of the fire.

Herbert Asquith (*English, 1852–1928*)

A VALENTINE FOR A LADY

Darling, at the Beautician's you buy
Your (a) hair
     (b) complexion
     (c) lips
     (d) dimples, &
     (e) teeth

For a like amount you could just as well buy a face.

Lucilius (Roman, first century A.D.*)*
TRANSLATED BY DUDLEY FITTS

UNTO MY VALENTINE

Unto my right well-beloved Valentine, John Paston,
Esq., be this bill delivered, etc.

Right reverend and worshipful and my right well-beloved Valentine, I recommend me unto you, full heartily desiring to hear of your welfare, which I beseech Almighty God long for to perserve unto His pleasure and your heart's desire. And if it please you to hear of my welfare, I am not in good health of body nor of heart, nor shall be till I hear from you.

For there wotteth no creature what pain that I endure,
And, for to be dead, I dare it not discure.

And my lady, my mother, hath labored the matter to my father full diligently, but she can no more get than ye know of, for the which God knoweth I am full sorry. But if ye love me, as I trust verily that ye do, ye will not leave me therefor. For if ye had not half the livelihood that ye have, for to do the greatest labor that any woman alive might, I would not forsake you.

And if ye command me to keep me true wherever I go,
Ywis I will do all my might you to love, and never no
    mo.
And if my friends say that I do amiss,
They shall not me let so for to do.
Mine heart me bids evermore to love you

Truly over all earthly thing,
And if they be never so wroth,
I trust it shall be better in time coming.

No more to you at this time, but the Holy Trinity
have you in keeping; and I beseech you that this bill
be not seen of none earthly creature save only yourself,
etc. And this letter was endited at Topcroft, with full
heavy heart, etc.

By your own
Margery Brews

Margery Brews (English, d. ca. 1495)

To-morrow is Saint Valentine's day,
   All in the morning betime,
And I a maid at your window,
   To be your Valentine.

Then up he rose, and donn'd his clothes,
   And dupp'd the chamber-door;
Let in the maid, that out a maid
   Never departed more.

William Shakespeare (English, 1564–1616)

FROM: AN EPITHALAMION,
or Marriage Song on The Lady
Elizabeth, and Count Palatine
Being Married on St. Valentine's
Day

I

Hail, Bishop Valentine, whose day this is,
    All the air is thy diocese,
    And all the chirping choristers
And other birds are thy parishioners,
    Thou marriest every year
The lyric Lark, and the grave whispering Dove,
The Sparrow that neglects his life for love,
The household Bird, with the red stomacher,
    Thou mak'st the Blackbird speed as soon
As doth the Goldfinch, or the Halcyon;
The husband cock looks out, and straight is sped,
And meets his wife, which brings her feather-bed.
This day, more cheerfully than ever shine,
This day, which might enflame thy self, Old Valentine.

John Donne (English, 1573–1631)

THE WOUNDED CUPID

Song.

Cupid as he lay among
Roses, by a Bee was stung.
Whereupon in anger flying
To his Mother, said thus crying;
Help! O help! your Boy's a dying.
And why, my pretty Lad, said she?
Then blubbering, replyed he,
A winged Snake has bitten me,
Which Country people call a Bee.
At which she smil'd; then with her hairs
And kisses drying up his tears:
Alas! said she, my Wag! if this
Such a pernicious torment is:
Come tell me then, how great's the smart
Of those, thou woundest with thy Dart!

Robert Herrick (English, 1591–1674)

TO HIS MISTRESSE

Choose me your Valentine;
    Next, let us marry:
Love to the death will pine,
    If we long tarry.

Promise, and keep your vowes,
    Or vow ye never:
Loves doctrine disallowes
    Troth-breakers ever.

You have broke promise twice
    (Deare) to undo me;
If you prove faithlesse thrice,
    None then will wooe ye.

Robert Herrick (*English, 1591–1674*)

From: SHEPHERDESS' VALENTINE

I bear, in sign of love,
A sparrow in my glove,
And in my breast a dove,
  These shall be all thine;
Besides, of sheep a flock,
Which yieldeth many a lock,
And that shall be thy stock—
  Come, be my valentine!

Francis Andrewes (English, fl. 1629–1643)

MY VALENTINE

I will make you brooches and toys for your delight
Of bird-song at morning and star-shine at night.
I will make a palace fit for you and me
   Of green days in forests and blue days at sea.

             Robert Louis Stevenson (*Scots, 1850–1894*)

VALENTINES TO MY MOTHER

1880

More shower than shine
Brings sweet St. Valentine;
Warm shine, warm shower,
Bring up sweet flower on flower.

Through shower and shine
Loves you your Valentine,
Through shine, through shower,
Through summer's flush,
Through autumn's fading hour.

Christina Rossetti (English, 1830–1894)

ST. VALENTINE

permitted to assist you, let me see . . .
   If those remembered by you
are to think of you and not me,
   it seems to me that the memento
   or compliment you bestow
should have a name beginning with "V,"

such as Vera, El Greco's only
   daughter (though it has never been
proved that he had one), her starchy
   veil, inside chiffon; the stone in her
   ring, like her eyes; one hand on
her snow-leopard wrap, the fur widely

dotted with black. It could be a vignette—
   a replica, framed oval—
bordered by a vine or vinelet.
   Or give a mere flower, said to mean the
   love of truth or truth of
love—in other words, a violet.

Verse—unabashedly bold—is appropriate;
   and always it should be as neat
as the most careful writer's "8."
   Any valentine that is *written*
Is as the *vendange* to the vine.
   Might verse not best confuse itself with fate?

Marianne Moore (American, 1887–1972)

Allhallows' Eve and Halloween

. . . Things that go bump in the Night

From Ghoulies and Ghosties,
And long-leggity Beasties,
And all Things that go bump in the Night,
Good Lord deliver us.

From a Cornish Litany

From: MACBETH, ACT IV, SCENE 1

FIRST WITCH

Thrice the brinded cat hath mew'd.

SECOND WITCH

Thrice and once the hedge-pig whined.

THIRD WITCH

Harpier cries 'Tis time, 'tis time.'

FIRST WITCH

Round about the cauldron go:
In the poison'd entrails throw.
Toad, that under cold stone
Days and nights has thirty one
Swelter'd venom sleeping got,
Boil thou first i' the charmed pot.

ALL

Double, double toil and trouble;
Fire burn and cauldron bubble.

SECOND WITCH

Fillet of a fenny snake,
In the cauldron boil and bake;
Eye of newt and toe of frog,

Wool of bat and tongue of dog,
Adder's fork and blind-worm's sting,
Lizard's leg and howlet's wing,
For a charm of powerful trouble,
Like a hell-broth boil and bubble.

ALL

Double, double toil and trouble;
Fire burn and cauldron bubble.

THIRD WITCH

Scale of dragon, tooth of wolf,
Witches' mummy, maw and gulf
Of the ravin'd salt-sea shark,
Root of hemlock digg'd i' the dark,
Liver of blaspheming Jew,
Gall of goat and slips of yew
Sliver'd in the moon's eclipse,
Nose of Turk and Tartar's lips,
Finger of birth-strangled babe
Ditch-deliver'd by a drab,
Make the gruel thick and slab:
Add thereto a tiger's chaudron,
For the ingredients of our cauldron.

ALL

Double, double toil and trouble;
Fire burn and cauldron bubble.

SECOND WITCH

Cool it with a baboon's blood,
Then the charm is firm and good.

William Shakespeare (English, 1564–1616)

From: THE MASQUE OF QUEENS

Hag.   What our Dame bids us do
            We are ready for.

Dame.   Then fall to.
           But first relate me what you have sought,
           Where you have been, and what you have
             brought.

1st Hag.   I have been all day looking after
           A raven feeding upon a quarter,
           And soon as she turned her beak to the
             south,
           I snatched this morsel out of her mouth.

2nd Hag.   I have been gathering wolves' hairs,
           The mad dogs' foam and the adders' ears,
           The spurging of a dead man's eyes,
           And all since the evening star did rise.

3rd Hag.   I last night lay all alone
           O' the ground to hear the mandrake
             groan,
           And plucked him up, though he grew full
             low,
           And as I had done, the cock did crow.

4th Hag.   And I ha' been choosing out this skull
           From charnel houses that were full,
           From private grots and public pits,
           And frightened a sexton out of his wits.

5th Hag.   Under a cradle I did creep
           By day, and when the child was asleep

At night I sucked the breath, and rose
And plucked the nodding nurse by the
nose.

6th Hag.   I had a dagger: what did I with that?
Killed an infant to have his fat.
A piper it got at a church-ale,
I bade him again blow wind i' the tail.

7th Hag.   A murderer yonder was hung in chains,
The sun and the wind had shrunk his
veins;
I bit off a sinew, I clipped his hair,
I brought off his rags that danced i' the
air.

8th Hag.   The scritch-owl's eggs and the feathers
black
The blood of the frog and the bone in his
back
I have been getting, and made of his skin
A purset to keep Sir Cranion in.

9th Hag.   And I ha' been plucking, plants among,
Hemlock, henbane, adder's tongue,
Nightshade, moonwort, libbard's bane,
And twice by the dogs was like to be
ta'en.

10th Hag.   I from the jaws of a gardener's bitch
Did snatch these bones, and then leaped
the ditch;

	Yet went I back to the house again,
	Killed the black cat, and here's the brain.
11th Hag.	I went to the toad breeds under the wall,
	I charmed him out and he came at my call;
	I scratched out the eyes of the owl before,
	I tore the bat's wing; what would you have more?
Dame.	Yes, I have brought, to help our vows,
	Hornèd poppy, cypress boughs,
	The fig-tree wild that grows on tombs,
	And juice that from the larch tree comes,
	The basilisk's blood and the viper's skin:
	And now, our orgies let's begin. . . .

Ben Jonson (English, 1573?–1637)

hist   whist
little ghostthings
tip-toe
twinkle-toe

little twitchy
witches and tingling
goblins
hob-a-nob   hob-a-nob

little hoppy happy
toad in tweeds
tweeds
little itchy mousies

with scuttling
eyes   rustle and run   and
hidehidehide
whisk

whisk   look out for the old woman
with the wart on her nose
what she'll do to yer
nobody knows

for she knows the devil   ooch
the devil   ouch
the devil
ach   the great

green
dancing

devil
devil

devil
devil

      wheeEEE

         e. e. cummings (American, 1894–1962)

INCANTATION TO OEDIPUS

Choose the darkest part o' the grove,
Such as ghosts at noon-day love.
Dig a trench, and dig it nigh
Where the bones of Laius lie;
Altars raised of turf or stone,
Will th' infernal powers have none.
Answer me, if this be done?
  'Tis done.
Is the sacrifice made fit?
Draw her backward to the pit:
Draw the barren heifer back;
Barren let her be, and black.
Cut the curled hair that grows
Full betwixt her horns and brows:
And turn your faces from the sun;
Answer me, if this be done?
  'Tis done.
Pour in blood, and blood-like wine,
To Mother Earth and Proserpine:
Mingle milk into the stream:
Feasts the ghosts that love the steam;
Snatch a brand from the funeral pile:
Toss it in, to make them boil:
And turn your faces from the sun;
Answer me, if this be done?
  'Tis done.

John Dryden (English, 1631–1700)

HALLOWEEN

Stealing white from the withered moon,
       dying breath from the wind,
       black eyes from the knobs of a wizened
oak,

     a ghost   soft gliding to my room
                 with sad moan,

                 looked,
                 listened long
                 to the sounds of silence,

                 cried,
                 then spoke:

"These I have seen, ten-thousand fold,
Other dark years—scampering rats,
Leering pumpkins, ghouls grown old
Groaning with evil, fiendish cats,
Witches, goblins, horrors yet untold.

Feasting and reveling Allhallows' Eve,
Flying off to a distant hill
Summoned by Satan; thus, they leave.
All harm is gone . . . Sleep long and well . . .
Hush, child, listen, and believe."

Myra Cohn Livingston (American, 1926–)

To Honor

Lincoln's Birthday

Up from the log cabin to the Capitol . . .

LINCOLN MONUMENT: WASHINGTON

Let's go see Old Abe
Sitting in the marble and the moonlight,
Sitting lonely in the marble and the moonlight,
Quiet for ten thousand centuries, old Abe.
Quiet for a million, million years.

Quiet—

And yet a voice forever
Against the
Timeless walls
Of time—
Old Abe.

Langston Hughes (*1902–1967*)

ANNE RUTLEDGE

Out of me, unworthy and unknown,
The vibrations of deathless music;
"With malice toward none, with charity for all."
Out of me the forgiveness of millions toward millions,
And the beneficent face of a nation
Shining with justice and truth.
I am Anne Rutledge who sleeps beneath these weeds,
Beloved in life of Abraham Lincoln,
Wedded to him, not through union,
But through separation.
Bloom forever, O Republic,
From the dust of my bosom!

Edgar Lee Masters (*American, 1869–1950*)

ABRAHAM LINCOLN WALKS AT MIDNIGHT

(In Springfield, Illinois)

It is portentous, and a thing of state
That here at midnight, in our little town
A mourning figure walks, and will not rest,
Near the old court-house pacing up and down,

Or by his homestead, or in shadowed yards
He lingers where his children used to play,
Or through the market, on the well-worn stones
He stalks until the dawn-stars burn away.

A bronzed, lank man! His suit of ancient black,
A famous high top-hat and plain worn shawl
Make him the quaint great figure that men love,
The prairie-lawyer, master of us all.

He cannot sleep upon his hillside now.
He is among us:—as in times before!
And we who toss and lie awake for long
Breathe deep, and start, to see him pass the door.

His head is bowed. He thinks of men and kings.
Yea, when the sick world cries, how can he sleep?
Too many peasants fight, they know not why,
Too many homesteads in black terror weep.

The sins of all the war-lords burn his heart.
He sees the dreadnaughts scouring every main.
He carries on his shawl-wrapped shoulders now
The bitterness, the folly and the pain.

He cannot rest until a spirit-dawn
Shall come;—the shining hope of Europe free:
The league of sober folk, the Workers' Earth,
Bringing long peace to Cornland, Alp and Sea.

It breaks his heart that kings must murder still,
That all his hours of travail here for men
Seem yet in vain. And who will bring white peace
That he may sleep upon his hill again?

Vachel Lindsay (American, 1879–1931)

From: LINCOLN, THE MAN OF THE PEOPLE

Up from the log cabin to the Capitol,
One fire was on his spirit, one resolve—
To send the keen ax to the root of wrong,
Clearing a free way for the feet of God,
The eyes of conscience testing every stroke,
To make his deed the measure of a man.
He built the rail-pile as he built the State,
Pouring his splendid strength through every blow:
The grip that swung the ax in Illinois
Was on the pen that set a people free. . . .

Edwin Markham, (American, 1852–1940)

II.

There was a darkness in this man; an immense and hol-
low darkness,
Of which we may not speak, nor share with him, nor
enter;
A darkness through which strong roots stretched down-
wards into the earth
Towards old things;
Towards the herdman-kings who walked the earth and
spoke with God,
Towards the wanderers who sought for they knew not
what, and found their goal at last;
Towards the men who waited, only waited patiently
when all seemed lost.
Many bitter winters of defeat;
Down to the granite of patience
Those roots swept, knotted fibrous roots, prying, pierc-
ing, seeking,
And drew from the living rock and the living waters
about it
The red sap to carry upwards to the sun.

John Gould Fletcher (*American, 1886–1950*)

From: EDGAR'S STORY

At Mount Rushmore I looked up into one
Of those faces born joined to the same neck bone.
I said, *Abe, Abe, how does it feel to be up there?*—
And that great rock he has for a pupil budged, I swear,
And he looked me in the eye and he said, *Alone.*

X. J. Kennedy (American, 1929–)

From: WHEN LILACS LAST IN THE DOORYARD BLOOM'D

When lilacs last in the dooryard bloom'd,
And the great star early droop'd in the western sky in the
   night,
I mourn'd, and yet shall mourn with ever-returning
   spring.

Ever-returning spring, trinity sure to me you bring,
Lilac blooming perennial and drooping star in the west,
And thought of him I love.

O powerful western fallen star!
O shades of night—O moody, tearful night!
O great star disappear'd—O the black murk that hides
   the star!
O cruel hands that hold me powerless—O helpless soul
   of me!
O harsh surrounding cloud that will not free my soul.

. . . . .

Coffin that passes through lanes and streets,
Through day and night with the great cloud darkening
   the land,
With the pomp of the inloop'd flags with the cities
   draped in black,
With the show of the States themselves as of crape-veil'd
   women standing,
With processions long and winding and the flambeaus
   of the night,

With the countless torches lit, with the silent sea of faces
and the unbared heads,
With the waiting depot, the arriving coffin, and the
sombre faces,
With dirges through the night, with the thousand voices
rising strong and solemn,
With all the mournful voices of the dirges pour'd
around the coffin,
The dim-lit churches and the shuddering organs—where
amid these your journey,
With the tolling tolling bells' perpetual clang,
Here, coffin that slowly passes,
I give you my sprig of lilac.

. . . . .

Walt Whitman (*American, 1819–1892*)

Washington's Birthday

Washington stands in marble
shaped from life . . .

WASHINGTON MONUMENT BY NIGHT

1

The stone goes straight.
A lean swimmer dives into night sky,
Into half-moon mist.

2

Two trees are coal black.
This is a great white ghost between.
It is cool to look at.
Strong men, strong women, come here.

3

Eight years is a long time
To be fighting all the time.

4

The republic is a dream.
Nothing happens unless first a dream.

5

The wind bit hard at Valley Forge one Christmas.
Soldiers tied rags on their feet.
Red footprints wrote on the snow . . .
. . . and stone shoots into stars here
. . . into half-moon mist tonight.

6

Tongues wrangled dark at a man.
He buttoned his overcoat and stood alone.
In a snowstorm, red hollyberries, thoughts,
      he stood alone.

7

Women said: He is lonely
. . . fighting . . . fighting . . . eight years . . .

8

The name of an iron man goes over the world.
It takes a long time to forget an iron man.

9

. . .   .
 . .   . .

Carl Sandburg (American, 1878–1967)

TO HIS EXCELLENCY
GEORGE WASHINGTON

Celestial choir! enthroned in realms of light,
  Columbia's scenes of glorious toils I write,
While freedom's cause her anxious breast alarms,
She flashes dreadful in refulgent arms.
See mother earth her offspring's fate bemoan,
And nations gaze at scenes before unknown!
See the bright beams of heaven's revolving light
Involved in sorrows and the veil of night!

  The goddess comes, she moves divinely fair,
Olive and laurel binds her golden hair:
Wherever shines this native of the skies,
Unnumbered charms and recent graces rise.

  Muse! bow propitious while my pen relates
How pour her armies through a thousand gates,
As when Eolus heaven's fair face deforms,
Enwrapped in tempest and a night of storms;
Astonished ocean feels the wild uproar,
The refluent surges beat the sounding shore;
Or thick as leaves in Autumn's golden reign,
Such, and so many, moves the warrior's train.
In bright array they seek the work of war,
Where high unfurled the ensign waves in air.
Shall I to Washington their praise recite?
Enough thou know'st them in the fields of fight.
Thee, first in peace and honours,—we demand
The grace and glory of thy martial band.
Famed for thy valour, for thy virtues more,

Hear every tongue thy guardian aid implore!
  One century scarce performed its destined round,
When Gallic powers Columbia's fury found;
And so may you, whoever dares disgrace
The land of freedom's heaven-defended race!
Fired are the eyes of nations on the scales,
For in their hopes Columbia's arm prevails.
Anon Brittannia droops the pensive head,
While round increase the rising hills of dead.
Ah! cruel blindness to Columbia's state!
Lament thy thirst of boundless power too late.
  Proceed, great chief, with virtue on thy side,
Thy ev'ry action let the goddess guide.
A crown, a mansion, and a throne that shine,
With gold unfading. Washington! be thine.

Phillis Wheatley (American, 1753?–1784)

PATRIOTIC POEM

George Washington, your name is on my lips.
You had a lot of slaves.
I don't like the idea of slaves. I know I am
a slave to
too many masters, already
a red cardinal flies out of the pine tree in my eye swoop-
    ing
down to crack a nut and the bird feeds on a tray draped
    with
a thirteen-starred flag. Underneath my heart where the
    fat clings
like bits of wool
I want to feel a man slipping his hand inside my body
massaging the heart, bathing
it in stripes, streams of new blood with stars floating in
    it
must pass through my arteries, each star pricking
the walls of veins with the prickly sensation of life.
The blood is old,
perhaps was shipped from Mt. Vernon
which was once a blood factory.
Mr. Washington, the pseudo aristocrat with two large
    fish instead of
feet, slapping around the plantation,
managing the country with surveyor's tools,
writing documents with sweet potatoes, yams, ham
    hocks, and black-eyed
peas,

oh I hate southern gentlemen, too bad he was one;
somehow I've always hated the men who ran my country
but I was a loyal citizen. "Take me to your leader,"
and I'll give him a transfusion of my AB negative blood
    with stars.
floating in it. I often said this
in a spirit of devotion, chauvinistic passion,
pining secretly for the beautiful Alexander Hamilton
    but making do with
George, who, after all, was the first president
and I need those firsts. On my wall, yes the wall of my
    stomach;
on my money, yes play money and real money, money I
    spend and money
I save, in and out of pocket; on documents, and deeds,
    statuary, monu–
ments, books, pictures, trains, old houses, whiskey bot-
    tles, and even
sewing machine shuttles there is his name
and my commitment, after all, is to names, how else, to
    what else
do we commit ourselves but names
and George I have committed myself to you. No
    Western sheriffs for me;
they only really like men and horses and sometimes gun
    play.
I guess I'm stuck with you, George, despite your ab-
    solute inability

to feel anything personal, or communicate it,
or at least share it with me.
Thank you at least for being first in your white linen
    and black coat.
My body, the old story, is my country, the only territory
    I control
and it certainly has been torn by wars. I'd like to think
    the
Revolution is over and that at last I am going to have
    my first pres–
ident, at last I can have an inaugural ball;
the white house of my corpuscles
asks for new blood; I have given so many transfusions to
    others.
When will you make me your first lady, George?
When will I finally become the first president's wife?

Diane Wakowski (American, 1937–)

WASHINGTON

Washington, the brave, the wise, the good,
Supreme in war, in council, and in peace,
Valiant without ambition, discreet without fear,
    Confident with presumption.

In disaster calm; in success, moderate; in all, himself.
The hero, the patriot, the Christian.
The father of nations, the friend of mankind,
Who, when had won all, renounced all,
Then sought in the bosom of his family and of
    nature, refinement,
And in the hope of religion, immortality.

Inscription at Mt. Vernon

MOUNT VERNON

What solemn sound the ear invades,
What wraps the land in sorrow's shade?
From heaven the awful mandate flies,
The Father of his country dies.

Where shall our country turn its eye,
What help remains beneath the sky?
Our friend, protector, strength, and trust,
Lies low and mould'ring in the dust.

Anonymous, American Folk

WASHINGTON'S MONUMENT,
FEBRUARY, 1885

Ah, not this marble, dead and cold:

Far from its base and shaft expanding—the round zones
  circling, comprehending,

Thou, Washington, art all the world's, the continents'
  entire—not yours alone, America,

Europe's as well, in every part, castle of lord or laborer's
  cot,

Or frozen North, or sultry South—the African's—the
  Arab's in his tent,

Old Asia's there with venerable smile, seated amid her
  ruins;

(Greets the antique the hero new? 'tis but the same—the
  heir legitimate, continued ever,

The indomitable heart and arm—proofs of the never-
  broken line,

Courage, alertness, patience, faith, the same—e'en in defeat defeated not, the same:)

Wherever sails a ship, or house is built on land, or day or
  night,

Through teeming cities' streets, indoors or out, factories
  or farms,

Now, or to come, or past—where patriot wills existed or
  exist,

Wherever Freedom, pois'd by Toleration, sway'd by
  Law,

Stands or is rising thy true monument.

Walt Whitman (American, 1819–1892)

JOLLY SOLDIER

I once was a seaman stout and bold,
Ofttimes I've ploughed the ocean;
I've ploughed it all o'er and o'er again,
For honor and promotion.

Aboard a man-of-war and merchantman,
Many be the battles that I've been in,
It was all for the honor of George Washington,
And I'll still be the jolly, jolly soldier.

Anonymous, American Folk

CONVERSATION WITH WASHINGTON

They did it, George. They did it.
                    What?
They changed your birthday quite a lot.
                         How?
They moved it to another day.
                    Why?
So they could have more time to play.
                         Where?
At lakes or mountains, or just rest—
                    When?
Some time ago. They thought it best.
                         Who?
Your children, George. They thought that you
Would understand. (Most fathers do—)

Myra Cohn Livingston (American, 1926–   )

Memorial, Veterans', and Armistice Day

*Remember that we died fighting
for what you are . . .*

THE DEATH OF A SOLDIER

Life contracts and death is expected,
As in a season of autumn.
The soldier falls.

He does not become a three-days personage,
Imposing his separation,
Calling for pomp.

Death is absolute and without memorial,
As in a season of autumn,
When the wind stops.

When the wind stops and, over the heavens,
The clouds go, nevertheless,
In their direction.

Wallace Stevens (American, 1879–1945)

"next to of course god america i
love you land of the pilgrims' and so forth oh
say can you see by the dawn's early my
country 'tis of centuries come and go
and are no more what of it we should worry
in every language even deafanddumb
thy sons acclaim your glorious name by gorry
by jingo by gee by gosh by gum
why talk of beauty what could be more beautiful than these heroic happy dead
who rushed like lions to the roaring slaughter
they did not stop to think they died instead
then shall the voice of liberty be mute?"

He spoke.   And drank rapidly a glass of water

e. e. cummings (*American, 1894–1962*)

VOICES OF HEROES

Overheard in a Churchyard Dedicated
to the Memory of 1776

"The cemetery stone New England autumn
Restores health to our voices,
Even our faces
Seem to reappear through gliding mist that gathers
In an unshuttered, moonlit, empty room.
We were the heroes, O wives, mothers, daughters!
Of war that lighted fires
Within these shores.

Open our graves: you will find nothing there
Unlike our common clay
That blows away,
Or mixed with water serves to build a wall;
But you might well imagine
That earth and air
Are relics of the True, Original Cross,
And that the trampled grass
Holds the imprint of Adam's image on this small hill—
Or you might say,
'Because their bones lie here,
The bleak earth glows with sunlight from their eyes;
They were the heroes
And their voices speak among us at their will.'

Yet too much praise leaves much unsaid:
Even in death we were, somehow, more human,

Moving among the shades of things we loved or hated,
Clasping the shadows of pretty girls, or restless women,
Or quarreling with a landlord,
Or gazing with regret at empty bottles,
Or shouldering old rifles,
Or for an hundred years (since we were freed from
    labor)
Playing at cards with a distrusted neighbor.
It is not true that we were always sad,
Or like evil, unquiet dead misspent our fury
Among cries of death at night in winter storms—
But the earthly spirit that fed our hearts had gone,
Gone with the vanished hope of richer farms,
Or brighter town, or countless money;
We had learned that there were no stakes to be won,
Even the unnamed, vital essence returned to God.

Now that another war flames in the east
 (We can see its fires reflected in the sky
And there are more than rumors in the air)
Remember that we died fighting for what you are—
Better to die
Than to sit watching the world die,
Better to sleep and learn at last
That terror and loss
Have not utterly destroyed us,
That even our naked shades
Still looked and talked like men—

That when we wake,
A little courage has earned our right to speak.
Remember that old wars remain unfinished,
As grass grows over earth, our names forgotten,
Or misread, misspelled in ivy-covered stone
With wreaths above our graves in summer's green—
Is that blaze the blaze of lightning from a cloud?
We do not fear them; we know that flesh is mortal
And in a world at war, only the wars live on."

Horace Gregory (American, 1898–   )

THE YOUNG DEAD SOLDIERS

for Lieutenant Richard Myers

The young dead soldiers do not speak.

Nevertheless, they are heard in the still houses: who has not heard them?

They have a silence that speaks for them at night and when the clock counts.

They say: We were young. We have died. Remember us.

They say: We have done what we could but until it is finished it is not done.

They say: We have given our lives but until it is finished no one can know what our lives gave.

They say: Our deaths are not ours; they are yours; they will mean what you make of them.

They say: Whether our loves and our deaths were for peace and a new hope or for nothing we cannot say; it is you who must say this.

They say: We leave you our deaths. Give them their meaning.

We were young, they say. We have died. Remember us.

Archibald MacLeish (American, 1892–)

A SIGHT IN CAMP IN THE DAYBREAK
GRAY AND DIM

A sight in camp in the daybreak gray and dim,
As from my tent I emerge so early sleepless,
As slow I walk in the cool fresh air the path near by the
hospital tent,
Three forms I see on stretchers lying, brought out there
untended lying,
Over each the blanket spread, ample brownish woolen
blanket,
Gray and heavy blanket, folding, covering all.

Curious I halt and silent stand,
Then with light fingers I from the face of the nearest the
first just lift the blanket;
Who are you elderly man so gaunt and grim, with well-
gray'd hair, and flesh all sunken about the eyes?
Who are you my dear comrade?

Then to the second I step—and who are you my child
and darling?
Who are you sweet boy with cheeks yet blooming?

Then to the third—a face nor child nor old, very calm, as
of beautiful yellow-white ivory;
Young man I think I know you—I think this face is the
face of the Christ himself,
Dead and divine and brother of all, and here again he
lies.

Walt Whitman (American, 1819–1892)

TO THE VETERANS OF THE
ABRAHAM LINCOLN BRIGADE

Say of them
They knew no Spanish
At first, and nothing of the arts of war
At first,
   how to shoot, how to attack, how to retreat
How to kill, how to meet killing
At first.
Say they kept the air blue
Grousing and griping.
Arid words and harsh faces. Say
They were young:
The haggard in a trench, the dead on the olive slope
All young. And the thin, the ill and the shattered,
Sightless, in hospitals, all young.

Say of them they were young, there was much they did
    not know,
They were human. Say it all: it is true. Now say
When the eminent, the great, the easy, the old,
And the men on the make
Were busy bickering and selling,
Betraying, conniving, transacting, splitting hairs,
Writing bad articles, signing bad papers,
Passing bad bills,
Bribing, blackmailing,
Whimpering, meaching, garroting,—they
Knew and acted
          understood and died.

Or if they did not die came home to peace
That is not peace.
                              Say of them
They are no longer young, they never learned
The arts, the stealth of peace, this peace, the tricks of
      fear;
And what they knew, they know.
And what they dared, they dare.

[1941]

Genevieve Taggard (American, 1894–1948)

THE SOLDIER

He is that fallen lance that lies as hurled,
That lies unlifted now, come dew, come rust,
But still lies pointed as it plowed the dust.
If we who sight along it round the world,
See nothing worthy to have been its mark,
It is because like men we look too near,
Forgetting that as fitted to the sphere,
Our missiles always make too short an arc.
They fall, they rip the grass, they intersect
The curve of earth, and striking, break their own;
They make us cringe for metal-point on stone.
But this we know, the obstacle that checked
And tripped the body, shot the spirit on
Further than target ever showed or shone.

Robert Frost (American, 1874–1963)

From: ELEGY FOR A DEAD SOLDIER

EPITAPH

Underneath this wooden cross there lies
A Christian killed in battle. You who read,
Remember that this stranger died in pain;
And passing here, if you can lift your eyes
Upon a peace kept by a human creed,
Know that one soldier has not died in vain.

New Guinea, 1944

Karl Shapiro (American, 1913–)

GUNNER

Did they send me away from my cat and my wife
To a doctor who poked me and counted my teeth,
To a line on a plain, to a stove in a tent?
Did I nod in the flies of the schools?

And the fighters rolled into the tracer like rabbits,
The blood froze over my splints like a scab—
Did I snore, all still and grey in the turret,
Till the palms rose out of the sea with my death?

And the world ends here, in the sand of a grave,
All my wars over? . . . It was easy as that!
Has my wife a pension of so many mice?
Did the medals go home to my cat?

Randall Jarrell (American, 1914–1965)

Fourth of July

. . . I stand free, knowing my land

FIREWORKS

Not guns, not thunder, but a flutter of clouded drums
That announce a fiesta: abruptly, fiery needles
Circumscribe on the night boundless chrysanthemums.
Softly, they break apart, they flake away, where
Darkness, on a svelte hiss, swallows them.
Delicate brilliance: a bellflower opens, fades,
In a sprinkle of falling stars.
Night absorbs them
With the sponge of her silence.

Babette Deutsch (American, 1895–   )

BRAVE NEW WORLD

But you, Thomas Jefferson,
You could not lie so still,
You could not bear the weight of stone
On the quiet hill,

You could not keep your green grown peace
Nor hold your folded hand
If you could see your new world now,
Your new sweet land.

There was a time, Tom Jefferson,
When freedom made free men.
The new found earth and the new freed mind
Were brothers then.

There was a time when tyrants feared
The new world of the free.
Now freedom is afraid and shrieks
At tyranny.

Words have not changed their sense so soon
Nor tyranny grown new.
The truths you held, Tom Jefferson,
Will still hold true.

What's changed is freedom in this age.
What great men dared to choose
Small men now dare neither win
Nor lose.

Freedom, when men fear freedom's use
But love its useful name,
Has cause and cause enough for fear
And cause for shame.

We fought a war in freedom's name
And won it in our own.
We fought to free a world and raised
A wall of stone.

Your countrymen who could have built
The hill fires of the free
To set the dry world all ablaze
With liberty—

To burn the brutal thorn in Spain
Of bigotry and hate
And the dead lie and the brittle weed
Beyond the Plate:

Who could have heaped the bloody straw,
The dung of time, to light
The Danube in a sudden flame
Of hope by night—

Your countrymen who could have hurled
Their freedom like a brand
Have cupped it to a candle spark
In a frightened land.

Freedom that was a thing to see
They've made a thing to save
And staked it in and fenced it round
Like a dead man's grave.

You, Thomas Jefferson,
You could not lie so still,
You could not bear the weight of stone
On your green hill,

You could not hold your angry tongue
If you could see how bold
The old stale bitter world plays new—
And the new world old.

Archibald MacLeish (American, 1892–   )

14

Now it's Uncle Sam sitting on top of the world.

Not so long ago it was John Bull, and, earlier yet, Napoleon, and the eagles of France told the world where to get off at.

Spain, Rome, Greece, Persia, their blunderbuss guns, their spears, catapults, ships, took their turn at leading the civilizations of the earth—

One by one they were bumped off, moved over, left behind, taken for a ride; they died or they lost the wallop they used to pack, not so good, not so good.

One by one they no longer sat on top of the world—now the Young Stranger is Uncle Sam, is America and the song goes, "The stars and stripes forever!" even though "forever" is a long time.

Even though the oldest kings had their singers and clowns calling, "Oh king, you shall live forever."

Carl Sandburg (American, 1878–1967)

TWILIGHT'S LAST GLEAMING

Higgledy-piggledy
President Jefferson
Gave up the ghost on the
Fourth of July.

So did John Adams, which
Shows that such patriots
Propagandistically
Knew how to die.

Arthur W. Monks (American, fl. Twentieth Century)

INDEPENDENCE DAY

for Gene Meatyard

Between painting a roof yesterday and the hay
harvest tomorrow, a holiday in the woods
under the grooved trunks and branches, the roof
of leaves lighted and shadowed by the sky.
As America from England, the woods stands free
from politics and anthems. So in the woods I stand
free, knowing my land. My country, tis of the
drying pools along Camp Branch I sing
where the water striders walk like Christ,
all sons of God, and of the woods grown old
on the stony hill where the thrush's song rises
in the light like a curling vine and the bobwhite's
whistle opens in the air, broad and pointed like a leaf.

Wendell Berry (American, 1934–   )

FOURTH OF JULY NIGHT

The little boat at anchor
in black water sat murmuring
to the tall black sky.

. . .

A white sky bomb fizzed on a black line.
A rocket hissed its red signature into the west.
Now a shower of Chinese fire alphabets,
a cry of flower pots broken in flames,
a long curve to a purple spray,
three violet balloons—
Drips of seaweed tangled in gold,
shimmering symbols of mixed numbers,
tremulous arrangements of cream gold folds
of a bride's wedding gown—

. . .

A few sky bombs spoke their pieces,
then velvet dark.

The little boat at anchor
in black water sat murmuring
to the tall black sky.

Carl Sandburg (American, 1878–1967)

Columbus Day

AND OF COLUMBUS

Columbus is remembered by young men
who walk the world at night in street-walled prisons:
Where is my country? Why do I return
at midnight to a moonlit, inland ocean
whose waves beat as a heart beats in my side?

Is the return to these receding shores
the end of earth, fallen to deep-sea traffic,
the end of all things?

The cities that coil upward
from sumac bush and sand flow into grass:
roofs, towers mingle
with roots and the bodies of men who died
in foreign wars.

       Columbus who believed his own miracles,
conquered his India, oceans, mermaids, golden savages—
where was his country?

It was a small stone room at night
in darkness. And time echoes time saying: Columbus no
    more,
where stars move toward the sun.

And in Havana under the Southern Cross, all that is his
is where his bones lie.

Horace Gregory (*American 1898–*)

THE DISCOVERY

There was an Indian, who had known no change,
Who strayed content along a sunlit beach
Gathering shells. He heard a sudden strange
Commingled noise; looked up, and gasped for speech.
For in the bay, where nothing was before,
Moved on the sea, by magic, huge canoes,
With bellying cloths on poles, and not one oar,
And fluttering colored signs and clambering crews.

And he, in fear, this naked man alone,
His fallen hands forgetting all their shells,
His lips gone pale, knelt low behind a stone,
And stared, and saw, and did not understand
Columbus' doom-burdened caravels
Slant to the shore, and all their seamen land.

John Collings Squire (*English, 1884–1958*)

COLUMBUS

Steer on, courageous sailor! Through mockery and jeer-
    ing
  while the skipper at the helm lowers a heedless hand.
Always, always westward! This is where the coast must
    loom
  as it lies clear and shimmering before your mind's eye.
Trust in the guiding God and follow the silent seas!
  If the coast was not there before, it would now rise
    from the waves.
Nature has an eternal pact with genius;
  What the one promises, the other will surely attain.

Friedrich von Schiller (German, 1759–1805)
TRANSLATED BY ERIKA GATHMANN KOESSLER

From: COLUMBUS

Chains, my good lord: in your raised brows I read
Some wonder at our chamber ornaments.
We brought this iron from our isles of gold.

Does the king know you deign to visit him
Whom once he rose from off his throne to greet
Before his people, like his brother king?
I saw your face that morning in the crowd.

At Barcelona—tho' you were not then
So bearded. Yes. The city deck'd herself
To meet me, roar'd my name; the king, the queen
Bade me be seated, speak, and tell them all
The story of my voyage, and while I spoke
The crowd's roar fell as at the "Peace, be still!"
And when I ceased to speak, the king, the queen,
Sank from their thrones, and melted into tears,
And knelt, and lifted hand and heart and voice
In praise to God who led me thro' the waste.
And then the great "Laudamus" rose to heaven.

Chains for the Admiral of the Ocean! chains
For him who gave a new heaven, a new earth,
As holy John had prophesied of me,
Gave glory and more empire to the kings
Of Spain than all their battles! chains for him
Who push'd his prows into the setting sun,
And made West East, and sail'd the Dragon's mouth,

And came upon the Mountain of the World,
And saw the rivers roll from Paradise!

    Chains! we are Admirals of the Ocean, we,
We and our sons for ever. Ferdinand
Hath sign'd it and our Holy Catholic queen—
Of the Ocean—of the Indies—Admirals we
Our title, which we never mean to yield,
Our guerdon not alone for what we did,
But our amends for all we might have done—
The vast occasion of our stronger life—
Eighteen long years of waste, seven in your Spain,
Lost, showing courts and kings a truth the babe
Will suck in with his milk hereafter—earth
A sphere.

              . . . . .

    All glory to the all-blessed Trinity,
All glory to the mother of our Lord.
And Holy Church, from whom I never swerved
Not even by one hair's-breadth of heresy,
I have accomplish'd what I came to do.

    Not yet—not all—last night a dream—I sail'd
On my first voyage, harass'd by the frights
Of my first crew, their curses and their groans.
The great flame-banner borne by Teneriffe,
The compass, like an old friend false at last
In our most need, appall'd them, and the wind

Still westward, and the weedy seas—at length
The landbird, and the branch with berries on it,
The carven staff—and last the light, the light
On Guanahani! but I changed the name;
San Salvador I call'd it; and the light
Grew as I gazed, and brought out a broad sky
Of dawning over—not those alien palms,
The marvel of that fair new nature—not
That Indian isle, but our most ancient East
Moriah with Jerusalem; and I saw
The glory of the Lord flash up . . .

· · · · ·

                          And God
Hath more than glimmer'd on me. O my lord,
I swear to you I heard his voice between
The thunders in the black Veragua nights,
"O soul of little faith, slow to believe?
Have I not been about thee from thy birth?
Given thee the keys of the great Ocean-sea?
Set thee in light till time shall be no more?
Is it I who have deceived thee or the world?
Endure! thou hast done so well for men, that men
Cry out against thee: was it otherwise
With mine own Son?"

                    And more than once in days
Of doubt and cloud and storm, when drowning hope
Sank all but out of sight, I heard his voice,

"Be not cast down. I lead thee by the hand,
Fear not." And I shall hear his voice again—
I know that he has led me all my life,
I am not yet too old to work his will—
His voice again.

                    Still for all that, my lord,
I lying here bedridden and alone,
Cast off, put by, scouted by court and king—
The first discoverer starves—his followers, all
Flower into fortune—our world's way—and I,
Without a roof that I can call mine own,
With scarce a coin to buy a meal withal,
And seeing what a door for scoundrel scum
I open'd to the West, thro' which the lust,
Villany, violence, avarice, of your Spain
Pour'd in on all those happy naked isles—
Their kindly native princes slain or slaved,
Their wives and children Spanish concubines,
Their innocent hospitalities quench'd in blood,
Some dead of hunger, some beneath the scourge,
Some over-labour'd, some by their own hands,—
Yea, the dear mothers, crazing Nature, kill
Their babies at the breast for hate of Spain—
Ah God, the harmless people whom we found
In Hispaniola's island-Paradise!
Who took us for the very Gods from Heaven,
And we have sent them very fiends from Hell;

And I myself, myself not blameless, I
Could sometimes wish I had never led the way.

     . . . . .

[chains . . .]
 You see that I have hung them by my bed,
And I will have them buried in my grave.

     . . . . .

Then some one standing by my grave will say,
"Behold the bones of Christopher Colòn"—
"Ay, but the chains, what do *they* mean—the chains?"—
I sorrow for that kindly child of Spain
Who then will have to answer, "These same chains
Bound these same bones back thro' the Atlantic sea,
Which he unchain'd for all the world to come."

     . . . . .

 Going? I am old and slighted: you have dared
Somewhat perhaps in coming? my poor thanks!
I am but an alien and a Genovese.

      Alfred, Lord Tennyson (English, 1809–1892)

MYSTERIOUS BIOGRAPHY

Christofo Colombo was a hungry man,
hunted himself half way round the world;
he began poor, panhandled, ended in jail,
Christofo so hungry, Christofo so poor,
Christofo in the chilly, steel bracelets,
honorable distinguished Christofo Colombo.

Carl Sandburg (American, 1878–1967)

COLUMBUS

Once upon a time there was an Italian,
And some people thought he was a rapscallion,
But he wasn't offended,
Because other people thought he was splendid,
And he said the world was round,
And everybody made an uncomplimentary sound,
But his only reply was Pooh,
He replied, Isn't this fourteen ninety-two?
It's time for me to discover America if I know my chro-
    nology,
And if I discover America you owe me an apology,
So he went and tried to borrow some money from Fer-
    dinand
But Ferdinand said America was a bird in the bush and
    he'd rather have a berdinand,
But Columbus' brain was fertile, it wasn't arid,
And he remembered that Ferdinand was married,
And he thought, there is no wife like a misunderstood
    one,
Because her husband thinks something is a terrible idea
    she is bound to think it a good one,
So he perfumed his handkerchief with bay rum and
    citronella,
And he went to see Isabella,
And he looked wonderful but he had never felt sillier,
And she said, I can't place the face but the aroma is
    familiar,
And Columbus didn't say a word,

All he said was, I am Columbus, the fifteenth-century
    Admiral Byrd,
And just as he thought, her disposition was very mal-
    leable,
And she said, Here are my jewels, and she wasn't
    penurious like Cornelia the mother of the Gracchi,
    she wasn't referring to her children, no, she was
    referring to her jewels, which were very very valuable,
So Columbus said, somebody show me the sunset and
    somebody did and he set sail for it,
And he discovered America and they put him in jail for
    it,
And the fetters gave him welts,
And they named America after somebody else,
So the sad fate of Columbus ought to be pointed out to
    every child and every voter,
Because it has a very important moral, which is, Don't
    be a discoverer, be a promoter.

Ogden Nash (American, 1902–1971)

THE ASSASSINATION

"Do you not find something very strange about him?"
Asked the First Fate,
"Very strange indeed," answered the Second Fate,
"He is immune to change."
"Yes, he is always young," complained the First Fate.
"He never heeds us," said the Second,
"I, for example, have often called and beckoned."
"We must kill him while he sleeps."
"He does not sleep."
"Then we must make him weep."
"He does not weep."
"Or laugh?"
"Only at his own epitaph,—
Half tears and laughter half."
"Then how to death that worst fate
To doom him?" said the First Fate.
"Oh, he's a clever one, as we've long reckoned,"
Answered the Second.
"But we can cope
With such a fellow, can we not,

What?"
"Could we not, say, with a falling girder
Carelessly cause an unintended murder?"
"Why not?"
"He's dead. Who said we could not cope
With this young fool. What was his name?"
"His name?"
"Of course that's not within our scope,
But just the same . . ."
"Hope was his name."
"How funny, Hope."

Robert Hillyer (American, 1895–1961)

ASSASSINATION POEMS

Not Believing It

The night is very dark
we see the cars moving
some by their lights
some by the darkening of the dark
and some cars moving without lights

Not Wanting to Believe It

That is the name of a far star:
Arcturus, it was written about.
Other stars too
have names, in constellations
one by one going out and
being born
"like fireflies in a summer night"

Knowing It

By the stream, squatting,
I try to slice
the water with my hands
into blocks, to lift them
into place, liquid blocks of clear water,
on the grass bank

The Assassin

And now we must begin to eat him:
we eat his hair, his lips, his eyelids,

his mother and father, his brothers,
his school friends, his buddies, his fiancées,
his minister, his employers, his books.
We eat everything we can find of his past,
we eat him in the present until we are stuffed full,
our gullets burning with all we have had to swallow,
guts bloating with the accumulation of his weeks and
    years.

The Friends

They turn to each other quickly
weaving a basket, trying to weave
a basket of words
watertight, greased to hold grief

The Nation

A house united by death
is a house of death

in which death is the head
of the house,

and we do as He says

John Ridland (American, 1933–   )

BOOTH KILLED LINCOLN

Wilkes Booth came to Washington, an actor great was
   he,
He played at Ford's Theater, and Lincoln went to see;
It was early in April, not many weeks ago,
The people of this fair city all gathered at the show.

The war it is all over, the people happy now,
And Abraham Lincoln arose to make his bow;
The people cheer him wildly, arising to their feet,
And Lincoln waving of his hand, he calmly takes his
   seat.

And while he sees the play go on, his thoughts are run-
   ning deep,
His darling wife, close by his side, has fallen fast asleep;
From the box there hangs a flag, it is not the Stars and
   Bars,
The flag that holds within its folds bright gleaming
   Stripes and Stars.

J. Wilkes Booth he moves down the aisle, he had mea-
   sured once before,
He passes Lincoln's bodyguard a-nodding at the door;
He holds a dagger in his right hand, a pistol in his left,
He shoots poor Lincoln in the temple, and sends his soul
   to rest.

The wife awakes from slumber, and screams in her rage,
Booth jumps over the railing, and lands him on the
   stage;

He'll rue the day, he'll rue the hour, as God him life
   shall give,
When Booth stood in the center stage, crying, "Tyrants
   shall not live!"

The people all excited then, cried everyone, "A hand!"
Cried all the people near, "For God's sake, save that
   man!"
Then Booth ran back with boot and spur across the
   backstage floor,
He mounts that trusty claybank mare, all saddled at the
   door.

J. Wilkes Booth, in his last play, all dressed in broad-
   cloth deep,
He gallops down the alleyway, I hear those horses' feet;
Poor Lincoln then was heard to say, and all has gone to
   rest,
"Of all the actors in this town, I loved Wilkes Booth the
   best."

Anonymous, American Folk Ballad

DOWN IN DALLAS

Down in Dallas, down in Dallas
Where the shadow of blood lies black,
Little Oswald nailed Jack Kennedy up
With the nail of a rifle crack.

The big bright Cadillacs stomped on their brakes,
The street fell unearthly still
While, smoke on its chin, that slithering gun
Coiled back from its window sill.

In a white chrome room on a table top
They tried all a scalpel knows,
But they couldn't spell stop to that drop-by-drop
Till it bloomed to a rigid rose.

Out on the altar, out on the altar
Christ blossoms in bread and wine,
But each asphalt stone where his blood dropped down
Is burst to a cactus spine.

Oh down in Dallas, down in Dallas
Where a desert wind walks by night,
He stood and they bound him foot and hand
To the cross of a rifle sight.

X. J. Kennedy (American, 1929–)

FOR MALCOLM: AFTER MECCA

My whole life has been a chronology of—*changes.*

You lie now in many coffins
in parlors where your name
is dropped more heavily even than Death
sent you crashing to the stage
on which you had exorcised our shame.

In little rooms they gather now
bringing their own memories of your pilgrimage
they come and go
speaking of revolution
without knowing as you learned
how static hate is
without recognizing the man you were
lay in our shame
and your growth to martyrdom.

Gerald W. Barrax (American, 1933–)

MALCOLM X

For Dudley Randall

Original
Ragged-round.
Rich-robust.

He had the hawk-man's eyes.
We gasped. We saw the maleness.
The maleness raking out and making guttural the air
and pushing us to walls.

And in a soft and fundamental hour
a sorcery devout and vertical
beguiled the world.

He opened us—
who was a key,

who was a man.

Gwendolyn Brooks (American, 1917–)

AARDVARK

Since
   Malcolm died
   That old aardvark
   has got a sort of fame
   for himself—
   I mean, of late, when I read
   The dictionary the first
   Thing I see
   Is that animal staring at me.
And then
   I think of Malcolm—
   How he read
   in the prisons
   And on the planes
   And everywhere
   And how he wrote
   About old Aardvark.
Looks like Malcolm X helped
Bring attention to a lot of things
We never thought about before.

Julia Fields (*American, 1938–*)

DEATH OF DR. KING

#1

we sit outside
the bars   the dime stores
everything is closed today

we are mourning
our hands filled with bricks
a brother is dead

my eyes are white and cold
water is in my hands

this is grief

#2

after the water
the broken bread
we return
to our separate
places

in our heads
bodies collapse
and grow again

the city boils
black men
jump out of trees

Sam Cornish (American, 1935–)

ASSASSINATION

it was wild
the
bullet hit high.
                    (the throat-neck)
& from everywhere:
          the motel, from under bushes and cars,
          from around corners and across streets,
          out of the garbage cans and from rat holes
          in the earth
they came running.
with
guns
drawn
they came running
toward the King—
          all of them
          fast and sure—

as *if*
the King
was going to fire back.
they came running,
fast and sure,
in the
wrong
direction.

Don L. Lee (American, 1942–)

To Remember

Easter

. . . the triumph of Golgotha

This Crosse-Tree   here
Doth   JESUS   beare,
Who   sweet'ned   first,
The   Death   accurs't.
Here all things ready are, make hast, make hast away;
For long this work will be, & very short this Day.
Why then, go on to act: Here's wonders to be done,
Before the last least sand of Thy ninth houre be run;
Or e're dark Clouds so dull, or dead the Mid-dayes Sun.
Act when Thou wilt,
Blood will be   spilt;
Pure Balm, that   shall
Bring   Health   to All.
Why   then,   Begin
To   powre   first   in
Some   Drops   of Wine
In   stead   of   Brine,
To search the   Wound,
So   long   unsound:
And when that's   done,
Let Oyle, next,   run,
To   cure   the   Sore
Sinne   made   before,

And O!   Deare Christ,
E'en as   Thou   di'st,
Look down,   and   see
Us   weepe   for   Thee.
And tho   (Love knows)
Thy   dreadful   Woes
Wee   cannot   ease;
Yet doe Thou   please,
Who   Mercie   art,
T'accept   each   Heart,
That   gladly   would
Helpe, if   it   could.
Meane while,   let mee,
Beneath   this   Tree,
This   Honour   have,
To   make   my   grave.

Robert Herrick (English, 1591–1674)

THE CHERRY-TREE CAROL

Joseph was an old man,
   And an old man was he,
And he married Mary,
   The Queen of Galilee.

Joseph and Mary walked
   Through an orchard good,
Where was cherries and berries,
   As red as any blood.

Joseph and Mary walked
   Through an orchard green,
Where was berries and cherries,
   As thick as might be seen.

O then bespoke Mary,
   So meek and so mild;
'Pluck me one cherry, Joseph,
   For I am with child.'

O then bespoke Joseph,
   With words most unkind:
'Let him pluck thee a cherry
   That brought thee with child.'

O then bespoke the babe,
   Within his mother's womb:
'Bow down then the tallest tree,
   For my mother to have some.'

Then bowed down the highest tree
    Unto his mother's hand;
Then she cried: 'See, Joseph,
    I have cherries at command.'

O then bespake Joseph:
    'I have done Mary wrong;
But cheer up, my dearest,
    And be not cast down.'

Then Mary plucked a cherry,
    As red as the blood,
Then Mary went home
    With her heavy load.

Then Mary took her babe,
    And sat him on her knee,
Saying: 'My dear son, tell me
    What this world will be.'

'O I shall be as dead, mother,
    As the stones in the wall;
O the stones in the streets, mother,
    Shall mourn for me all.

'Upon Easter-day, mother,
    My uprising shall be;
O the sun and the moon, mother,
    Shall both rise with me.'

Traditional English Carol

LITTLE CATKINS

Little boys and little maidens
Little candles, little catkins
    Homeward bring.

Little lights are burning softly,
People cross themselves in passing—
    Scent of spring.

Little wind so bold and merry,
Little raindrops, don't extinguish
    These flames, pray!

I will rise tomorrow, early,
Rise to greet you, Willow Sunday,
    Holy day.

Alexander Blok (*Russian, 1880–1921*)
TRANSLATED BY BABETTE DEUTSCH

THE LAST SUPPER

They are gathered, astounded and disturbed,
round him who, like a sage resolved to his end,
takes himself away from those he belonged to,
and who alien past them flows.
The old loneliness comes over him
that reared him to the doing of his deep acts;
now again will he wander through the olive grove,
and those who love him will take flight before him.

He has summoned them to the last supper
and (as a shot scatters birds out of the sheaves)
he scatters their hands from among the loaves
with his word: they fly across to him;
they flutter anxious through the table's round
and try to find a way out. But he
is everywhere like a twilight-hour.

Rainer Maria Rilke (*German, 1875–1926*)
TRANSLATED BY M. D. HERTER NORTON

CALVARY

Friendless and faint, with martyred steps and slow,
Faint for the flesh, but for the spirit free,
Stung by the mob that came to see the show,
The Master toiled along to Calvary.
We gibed him, as he went, with houndish glee,
Till his dimmed eyes for us did overflow;
We cursed his vengeless hands thrice wretchedly—
And this was nineteen hundred years ago.

But after nineteen hundred years the shame
Still clings, and we have not made good the loss
That outraged faith has entered in his name.
Ah, when shall come love's courage to be strong!
Tell me, O Lord—tell me, O Lord, how long
Are we to keep Christ writhing on the cross!

Edwin Arlington Robinson (American, 1869–1935)

PIETA

Now is my misery full, and namelessly
it fills me. I am stark, as the stone's
inside is stark.
Hard as I am, I know but one thing:
You grew—
. . . and grew
in order to stand forth
as too great pain
quite beyond my heart's grasping.
Now you are lying straight across my lap,
now I can no longer
give you birth.

Rainer Maria Rilke (*German, 1875–1926*)
TRANSLATED BY M. D. HERTER NORTON

EASTER SUNDAY

Last night did Christ the Sun rise from the dark,
  The mystic harvest of the fields of God,
And now the little wandering tribes of bees
  Are brawling in the scarlet flowers broad.
The winds are soft with birdsong; all night long
  Darkling the nightingale her descant told,
And now inside church doors the happy folk
  The Alleluia chant a hundredfold.
O Father of thy folk, be thine by right
The Easter joy, the threshold of the light.

Sedulius Scottus (Roman, 848–874)
TRANSLATED BY HELEN WADDELL

EASTER COMMUNION

Pure fasted faces draw unto this feast:
God comes all sweetness to your Lenten lips.
You striped in secret with breath-taking whips,
Those crooked rough-scored chequers may be pieced
To crosses meant for Jesus; you whom the East
With draught of thin and pursuant cold so nips
Breathe Easter now; you serged fellowships,
You vigil-keepers with low flames decreased.

God shall o'er-brim the measures you have spent
With oil of gladness; for sackcloth and frieze
And the ever-fretting shirt of punishment
Give myrrhy-threaded golden folds of ease.
Your scarce-sheathed bones are weary of being bent:
Lo, God shall strengthen all the feeble knees.

Gerard Manley Hopkins (*English, 1844–1889*)

EASTER HYMN

If in that Syrian garden, ages slain,
You sleep, and know not you are dead in vain,
Not even in dreams behold how dark and bright
Ascends in smoke and fire by day and night
The hate you died to quench and could but fan,
Sleep well and see no morning, son of man.

But if, the grave rent and the stone rolled by,
At the right hand of majesty on high
You sit, and sitting so remember yet
Your tears, your agony and bloody sweat,
Your cross and passion and the life you gave,
Bow hither out of heaven and see and save.

A. E. Housman (English, 1859–1936)

BALLAD OF THE GOODLY FERE

Simon Zelotes speaketh it somewhile
after the Crucifixion
                    Fere = Mate, Companion

Ha' we lost the goodliest fere o' all
For the priests and the gallows tree?
Aye lover he was of brawny men,
O' ships and the open sea.

When they came wi' a host to take Our Man
His smile was good to see,
"First let these go!" quo' our Goodly Fere,
"Or I'll see ye damned," says he.

Aye he sent us out through the crossed high spears
And the scorn of his laugh rang free,
"Why took ye not me when I walked about
Alone in the town?" says he.

Oh we drunk his "Hale" in the good red wine
When we last made company,
No capon priest was the Goodly Fere
But a man o' men was he.

I ha' seen him drive a hundred men
Wi' a bundle o' cords swung free,
That they took the high and holy house
For their pawn and treasury.

They'll no' get him a' in a book I think
Though they write it cunningly;
No mouse of the scrolls was the Goodly Fere
But aye loved the open sea.

If they think they ha' snared our Goodly Fere
They are fools to the last degree.
"I'll go to the feast," quo' our Goodly Fere,
"Though I go to the gallows tree."

"Ye ha' seen me heal the lame and blind,
And wake the dead," says he,
"Ye shall see one thing to master all;
'Tis how a brave man dies on the tree."

A son of God was the Goodly Fere
That bade us his brothers be.
I ha' seen him cow a thousand men.
I have seen him upon the tree.

He cried no cry when they drave the nails
And the blood gushed hot and free,
The hounds of the crimson sky gave tongue
But never a cry cried he.

I ha' seen him cow a thousand men
On the hills o' Galilee,
They whined as he walked out calm between,
Wi' his eyes like the grey o' the sea,

Like the sea that brooks no voyaging
With the winds unleashed and free,
Like the sea that he cowed at Genseret
W' twey words spoke' suddently.

A master of men was the Goodly Fere,
A mate of the wind and sea,
If they think they ha' slain our Goodly Fere
They are fools eternally.

I ha' seen him eat o' the honey-comb
Sin' they nailed him to the tree.

Ezra Pound (*American, 1885–1972*)

RESURRECTION

Some of us
these days
will kneel before altars
resplendent with cloth and gold
redolent with incense
exalted by homage
to a Jew
crucified, dead and buried
—Forgive them, Father, they know not what they do—
who rose from the tomb
with nail holes in His hands and feet
and spear in His side
to teach us
that love conquers all . . .

And others of us
will sit around the family table
lift high the cup of wine
and answer four questions
in homage to Jehovah
and Moses
for delivering us in the exodus
out of bondage in Egypt
into the promised land
to live in freedom and light
under the laws of the prophets . . .

And then
there are some of us—
—sons and daughters of Ham
—they say
who still toil under the yoke
of bondage and oppression
in a dark and weary land . . .
sometimes we wonder
in anguish—
where is He
that brings love and freedom?
—why hast thou forsaken me—
where is Moses
to strike off our chains
and lead us into the promised land?

But that still small voice
is thundering louder and louder:
Love ye all men
—yeah even Ross Barnett
    and Faubus and Bull Connor
Love ye all men . . .
and you yourself
press against the yoke
with ballots
and dignity
—and holes in hands and feet
and compassion

even for him
who wields the lash—
—they know not what they do—
and you may save his soul
and theirs that break unleavened bread
—for you were strangers in the land of Egypt
and theirs that eat of His Body and Blood
—love thy neighbor as thyself
and your own
as you impel the world to recall
the triumph of Golgotha
and the glory of love
and the laws of the prophets.

Frank Horne (American, 1899–1974)

Thanksgiving

Enter into His gates with thanksgiving . . .

THANKSGIVING

Thanksgiving for a former, doth invite
God to bestow a second benefit.

Robert Herrick (English, 1591–1674)

AROUND THANKSGIVING

(Englyn Milwr)

Pure gold, they said in her praise:
So I walk my autumn ways,
Around me a golden haze.

From the ground, in leaves, in air—
Oh, everywhere, everywhere!—
To save, to spend, and to share.

By the door, with evening light,
Westering, lingering late
Over lane and lawn and lot

The leaves of the lilac hold
The shape of the heart, *pure gold,*
As if I need to be told,

As if I need reminding,
Toward chill November's ending,
Of warmth and love abounding.

Rolfe Humphries (American, 1894–1969)

PSALM 100

A Psalm of Praise

Make a joyful noise unto the Lord, all ye lands.

Serve the Lord with gladness: come before his presence with singing.

Know ye that the Lord he is God: it is he that hath made us, and not we ourselves: we are his people, and the sheep of his pasture.

Enter into his gates with thanksgiving, and into his courts with praise: be thankful unto him, and bless his name.

For the Lord is good; his mercy is everlasting; and his truth endureth to all generations.

The Holy Bible: King James Version

I WILL GO WITH MY FATHER
A-PLOUGHING

I will go with my father a-ploughing
To the green field by the sea,
And the rooks and crows and sea-gulls
Will come flocking after me.
I will sing to the patient horses,
With the lark in the white of the air,
And my father will sing the plough-song
That blesses the cleaving share.

I will go with my father a-sowing
To the red field by the sea,
And the rooks and the gulls and the starlings
Will come flocking after me.
I will sing to the striding sowers
With the finch on the greening sloe,
And my father will sing the seed-song
That only the wise men know.

I will go with my father a-reaping
To the brown field by the sea,
And the geese and the crows and the children
Will come flocking after me.
I will sing to the tan-faced reapers,
With the wren in the heat of the sun,
And my father will sing the scythe-song
That joys for the harvest done.

Joseph Campbell (Irish, 1879–1944)

HARVEST SONG

O reapers and gleaners,
Come dance in the sun:
The last sheaves are stooked,
And the harvest is done.

The thistle-finch sings,
And the corn-plover cries,
And the bee and the moth
Flit about in the skies.

For Jesus has quickened
The seed in the mould,
And turned the green ears
Of the summer to gold.

The hill-folk all winter
Have clamoured for bread,
And here is enough
For a host to be fed!

Last year was a lean year,
And this is a fat,
And poor folk have cause
To be thankful for that.

So, reapers and gleaners,
Come dance in the sun,
And praise Mary's Child
That the harvest is done.

Joseph Campbell (*Irish, 1879–1944*)

THANKSGIVING

In childhood you think
This will go on forever.
Your elders are talking.
You do not understand.

They are eating pounds
Of the light and the dark.
The bottle is moving.
It passes from hand to hand.
It leans to every glass.
This will go on forever.
The hour will never pass.

At the end of the wine,
Leaving the others talking,
One by one they slip away
To their invisible beds.

Now you are alone.
The bones are clean.
The bottle is empty.
You take the last sip
They leave in every glass.
This meal will never end.

John N. Morris (English, 1931–)

A THANKSGIVING TO GOD, FOR HIS HOUSE

Lord, Thou has given me a cell
      Wherein to dwell;
A little house, whose humble roof
      Is weather-proof;
Under the sparres of which I lie
      Both soft, and drie;
Where Thou my chamber for to ward
      Hast set a Guard
Of harmlesse thoughts, to watch and keep
      Me, while I sleep.
Low is my porch, as is my Fate,
      Both void of state;
And yet the threshold of my doore
      Is worn by'th poore,
Who thither come, and freely get
      Good words, or meat:
Like as my Parlour, so my Hall
      And Kitchin's small:
A little Butterie, and therein
      A little Byn,
Which keeps my little loaf of Bread
      Unchipt, unflead:
Some brittle sticks of Thorne or Briar
      Make me a fire,
Close by whose living coale I sit,
      And glow like it.

Lord, I confesse too, when I dine,
      The Pulse is Thine,
And all those other Bits, that bee
      There plac'd by Thee;
The Worts, the Purslain, and the Messe
      Of Water-cresse,
Which of Thy kindnesse Thou hast sent;
      And my content
Makes those, and my beloved Beet,
      To be more sweet.
'Tis Thou that crown'st my glittering Hearth
      With guiltlesse mirth;
And giv'st me Wassaile Bowles to drink,
      Spic'd to the brink.
Lord, 'tis thy plenty-dropping hand,
      That soiles my land;
And giv'st me, for my Bushell sowne,
      Twice ten for one:
Thou mak'st my teeming Hen to lay
      Her egg each day:
Besides my healthfull Ewes to beare
      Me twins each yeare:
The while the conduits of my Kine
      Run Creame, (for Wine.)
All these, and better Thou dost send
      Me, to this end,

That I should render, for my part,
     A thankfull heart;
Which, fir'd with incense, I resigne,
     As wholly Thine;
But the acceptance, that must be,
     My Christ, by Thee.

Robert Herrick (English, 1591–1674)

PRAYER FOR THE GREAT FAMILY

Gratitude to Mother Earth, sailing through night and
     day—
    and to her soil: rich, rare, and sweet
        in our minds so be it.

Gratitude to Plants, the sun-facing light-changing leaf
    and fine root-hairs; standing still through wind
    and rain; their dance is in the flowing spiral grain
        in our minds so be it.

Gratitude to Air, bearing the soaring Swift and the
     silent
    Owl at dawn. Breath of our song
    clear spirit breeze
        in our minds so be it.

Gratitude to Wild Beings, our brothers, teaching secrets,
    freedoms and ways; who share with us their milk;
    self-complete, brave, and aware
        in our minds so be it.

Gratitude to Water: clouds, lakes, rivers, glaciers;
    holding or releasing; streaming through all
    our bodies salty seas
        in our minds so be it.

Gratitude to the Sun: blinding pulsing light through
    trunks of trees, through mists, warming caves where
    bears and snakes sleep—he who wakes us—
        in our minds so be it.

Gratitude to the Great Sky
    who holds billions of stars—and goes yet beyond
        that—
    beyond all powers, and thoughts
    and yet is within us—
    Grandfather Space.
    The Mind is his Wife.

        so be it.

                after a Mohawk prayer

            Gary Snyder (American, 1930–)

Christmas

Christmas comes like this . . .

Some say that ever 'gainst that season comes
Wherein our Saviour's birth is celebrated,
The bird of dawning singeth all night long:
And then, they say, no spirit dare stir abroad,
The nights are wholesome, then no planets strike,
No fairy tale nor witch hath power to charm,
So hallow'd and so gracious is the time.

William Shakespeare (English, 1564–1616)

A CHRISTMAS HYMN

> *And some of the Pharisees from among*
> *the multitude said unto him, Master, rebuke*
> *thy disciples.*
>
> *And he answered and said unto them, I*
> *tell you that, if these should hold their peace,*
> *the stones would immediately cry out.*
>
> ST. LUKE XIX, 39–40

A stable-lamp is lighted
Whose glow shall wake the sky;
The stars shall bend their voices,
And every stone shall cry.
And every stone shall cry,
And straw like gold shall shine;
A barn shall harbor heaven,
A stall become a shrine.

This child through David's city
Shall ride in triumph by;
The palm shall strew its branches,
And every stone shall cry.
And every stone shall cry,
Though heavy, dull, and dumb,
And lie within the roadway
To pave his kingdom come.

Yet he shall be forsaken
And yielded up to die;
The sky shall groan and darken,

And every stone shall cry.
And every stone shall cry
For stony hearts of men:
God's blood upon the spearhead,
God's love refused again.

But now, as at the ending,
The low is shifted high:
The stars shall bend their voices,
And every stone shall cry.
And every stone shall cry
In praises of the child
By whose descent among us
The worlds are reconciled.

Richard Wilbur (American, 1921–)

TO A YOUNG WRETCH

(Boethian)

As gay for you to take your father's ax
As take his gun—rod—to go hunting—fishing.
You nick my spruce until its fiber cracks,
It gives up standing straight and goes down swishing.
You link an arm in its arm and you lean
Across the light snow homeward smelling green.

I could have bought you just as good a tree
To frizzle resin in a candle flame,
And what a saving 'twould have meant to me.
But tree by charity is not the same
As tree by enterprise and expedition.
I must not spoil your Christmas with contrition.

It is your Christmases against my woods.
But even where, thus, opposing interests kill,
They are to be thought of as opposing goods
Oftener than conflicting good and ill;
Which makes the war god seem no special dunce
For always fighting on both sides at once.

And though in tinsel chain and popcorn rope
My tree a captive in your window bay,
Has lost its footing on my mountain slope
And lost the stars of heaven, may, oh, may
The symbol star it lifts against your ceiling
Help me accept its fate with Christmas feeling.

Robert Frost (*American, 1874–1963*)

A MAIDEN THAT IS MAKELESS

I sing of a maiden.
    That is makeless.
King of all Kings
    To her son she chose.

He came all so stille
    There his mother was
As dew in Aprille
    That falleth on the grass.

He came all so stille
    To his mother's bower
As dew in Aprille
    That falleth on the flower.

He came all so stille
    There his mother lay,
As dew in Aprille
    That falleth on the spray.

Mother and maiden
    Was never none but she;
Well may such a lady
    Godes mother be.

Traditional English, Fifteenth Century

COVENTRY CAROL

Lully, lulla, thou little tiny child,
By by, lully lullay.
O sisters too,
How may we do
 For to preserve this day
This poor youngling
For whom we do sing,
 By by, lully lullay?

Herod the king,
In his raging,
 Chargèd he hath this day
His men of might,
In his own sight,
 All young childrén to slay.

That woe is me,
Poor child for thee!
 And ever morn and day,
For thy parting
Neither say nor sing
 By by, lully lullay!

From, Pageant of the Shearmen and Tailors,
English, Fifteenth Century

CHRISTMAS 1959 ET CETERA

Where is the star of Bethlehem?
Oh God
Vanguard has eclipsed it!
There is the star of Bethlehem—
dimly between
Sputnik
&
Pioneer

Where are the carols of Christmas?
listen
the earth carols
diminuendo
the heavens
crescendo

These are the carols of Christmas—
"Upon a midnight clear . . .
beep . . . beep . . . beeP
"Silent night, holy night. . .
beep . . . beep . . . beEP
"Christ the savior is born . . .
beep . . . bEEP . . . bEEP
joy to the . . .
bEEP . . . bEEP
joy . . .
BEEP!

Gerald William Barrax (American, 1933–   )

THE MAGI

Now as at all times I can see in the mind's eye,
In their stiff, painted clothes, the pale unsatisfied ones
Appear and disappear in the blue depth of the sky
With all their ancient faces like rain-beaten stones,
And all their helms of silver hovering side by side,
And all their eyes still fixed, hoping to find once more,
Being by Calvary's turbulence unsatisfied,
The uncontrollable mystery on the bestial floor.

William Butler Yeats (*Irish, 1865–1935*)

KARMA

Christmas was in the air and all was well
With him, but for a few confusing flaws
In divers of God's images. Because
A friend of his would neither buy nor sell,
Was he to answer for the axe that fell?
He pondered; and the reason for it was,
Partly, a slowly freezing Santa Claus
Upon the corner, with his beard and bell.

Acknowledging an improvident surprise,
He magnified a fancy that he wishes
The friend whom he had wrecked were here again.
Not sure of that, he found a compromise;
And from the fulness of his heart he fished
A dime for Jesus who had died for men.

Edwin Arlington Robinson (American, 1869–1935)

THE HOLLY AND THE IVY

The holly and the ivy,
When they are both full grown,
Of all the trees that are in the wood,
The holly bears the crown:

> *The rising of the sun*
> *And the running of the deer,*
> *The playing of the merry organ,*
> *Sweet singing in the choir.*

The holly bears a blossom,
As white as the lily flower,
And Mary bore sweet Jesus Christ,
To be our sweet Saviour:

The holly bears a berry,
As red as any blood,
And Mary bore sweet Jesus Christ
To do poor sinners good:

The holly bears a prickle,
As sharp as any thorn,
And Mary bore sweet Jesus Christ
On Christmas day in the morn:

The holly bears a bark,
As bitter as any gall,
And Mary bore sweet Jesus Christ
For to redeem us all:

The holly and the ivy,
When they are both full grown,
Of all the trees that are in the wood,
The holly bears the crown:

Traditional English

THE CULTIVATION OF
CHRISTMAS TREES

There are several attitudes towards Christmas,
Some of which we may disregard:
The social, the torpid, the patently commercial,
The rowdy (the pubs being open till midnight),
And the childish—which is not that of the child
For whom the candle is a star, and the gilded angel
Spreading its wings at the summit of the tree
Is not only a decoration, but an angel.
The child wonders at the Christmas Tree:
Let him continue in the spirit of wonder
At the Feast as an event not accepted as a pretext;
So that the glittering rapture, the amazement
Of the first-remembered Christmas Tree,
So that the surprises, delight in new possessions
 (Each one with its peculiar and exciting smell),
The expectation of the goose or turkey
And the expected awe on its appearance,
So that the reverence and the gaiety
May not be forgotten in later experience,
In the bored habituation, the fatigue, the tedium,
The awareness of death, the consciousness of failure,
Or in the piety of the convert
Which may be tainted with a self-conceit
Displeasing to God and disrespectful to the children
(and here I remember also with gratitude
St. Lucy, her carol, and her crown of fire):
So that before the end, the eightieth Christmas

(By "eightieth" meaning whichever is the last)
The accumulated memories of annual emotion
May be concentrated into a great joy
Which shall be also a great fear, as on the occasion
When fear came upon every soul
Because the beginning shall remind us of the end
And the first coming of the second coming.

T. S. Eliot (American, 1888–1965)

Other Religious Holidays
. . . *come up in pilgrimage*

FROM: ORAGA HARU

Buddha's Birthday: April 8, 1819

Person after person
Pours sweet tea
Over the Buddha newborn
This long April day.

Today
Must be a holiday
Even
For the long rain.

Buddha's Death Day: February 15, 1815

In silence I lie
Like the Buddha
Aloof, though disturbed
By the flowers.

Even asleep
Buddha accepts
The money
And the flowers.

Issa (Japanese, 1763–1827)
TRANSLATED BY NOBUYUKI YUASA

A TRUE LENT

Is this a fast, to keep
    The larder lean
      And clean
From fat of veals and sheep?

Is it to quit the dish
    Of flesh, yet still
      To fill
The platter high with fish?

Is it to fast an hour,
    Or ragged to go,
      Or show
A downcast look and sour?

No: 'tis a fast to dole
    Thy sheaf of wheat
      And meat
Unto the hungry soul.

It is to fast from strife
    From old debate
      And hate;
To circumcise thy life.

To show a heart grief-rent;
    To starve thy sin,
      Not bin:
And that's to keep thy Lent.

Robert Herrick (*English, 1591–1674*)

HOLY THURSDAY

'Twas on a Holy Thursday, their innocent faces clean,
The children walking two and two, in red and blue and
green,
Grey-bearded beadles walk'd before, with wands as
white as snow,
Till into the high dome of Paul's they like Thames'
waters flow.

O what a multitude they seem'd, these flowers of
London town!
Seated in companies they sit with radiance all their own.
The hum of multitudes was there, but multitudes of
lambs,
Thousands of little boys and girls raising their innocent
hands.

Now like a mighty wind they raise to heaven the voice of
song,
Or like harmonious thunderings the seats of heaven
among.
Beneath them sit the aged men, wise guardians of the
poor;
Then cherish pity, lest you drive an angel from your
door.

William Blake (English, 1757–1827)

GOOD FRIDAY

Am I a stone and not a sheep
    That I can stand, O Christ, beneath Thy Cross,
    To number drop by drop Thy Blood's slow loss,
And yet not weep?

Not so those women loved
    Who with exceeding grief lamented Thee;
    Not so fallen Peter weeping bitterly;
Not so the thief was moved;

Not so the Sun and Moon
    Which hid their faces in a starless sky,
A horror of great darkness at broad noon,—
    I, only I.

Yet give not o'er,
    But seek Thy sheep, true Shepherd of the flock;
Greater than Moses, turn and look once more
    And smite a rock.

Christina Rossetti (*English, 1830–1894*)

PIYYUT FOR ROSH HASHANA

For this is not the road against which stand enemy lines,
   or foreign languages,
Or muteness.
Neither I nor my voice is tied by the conditions set on
   these distances.
I walk and I am not murdered.
I come at last to the house. I stop. I knock at the door.

All men who forgive say, What has been has been. I re-
   peat it.
All women who forgive stand on the porches sooner or
   later.
There is a window which is not black. There is a letter
   which is not lost on the way.
And if it did not arrive yesterday, it will surely arrive
   tomorrow.

All the cities are open tonight. None is beseiged or em-
   balmed.
Guests will arrive tonight and I am one of them.
In all the windows, branches of regret are opening one
   after another.
Many words come up in pilgrimage from lands of silence
   and death.

The curtains billow and the doors move on their hinges.

Chaim Guri (Israeli, 1923–)
TRANSLATED BY RUTH FINER MINTZ

This is the autumn and our harvest—
such as it is, such as it is—
the beginnings of the end, bare trees and barren ground;
but for us only the beginning:
let the wild goat's horn
and the silver trumpet sound!

Reason upon reason
to be thankful:
for the fruit of the earth,
for the fruit of the tree,
for the light of the fire,
and to have come to this season.

The work of our hearts is dust
to be blown about in the winds
by the God of our dead in the dust
but our Lord delighting in life
 (let the wild goat's horn
and the silver trumpet sound!) —
our God Who imprisons in coffin and grave
and unbinds the bound.

Charles Reznikoff (American, 1894–1976)

YOM KIPPUR: FASTING

The appetite
stirs. On this one day
at the year's end
the head becomes light

of blandishment of palate,
without embroideries of tongue or hand.
Saliva drying, your body
is a transparent cave.

You can see
through the skull into the brain's cavity.
You are a harp for whatever wind
God wants to play.

His music sounds sharper. There is no
barrier between his thought and you.

Ruth Whitman (American, 1922–)

Then they took whole stones according to the law, and built a new altar according to the former:

And they built up the holy places, and the things that were within the temple: and they sanctified the temple, and the courts.

And they made new holy vessels, and brought in the candlestick, and the altar of incense, and the table into the temple.

And they put incense upon the altar, and lighted up the lamps that were upon the candlestick, and they gave light in the temple.

And they set the loaves upon the table, and hung up the veils, and finished all the works that they had begun to make.

And they arose before the morning on the five and twentieth day of the ninth month (which is the month of Casleu) in the hundred and forty-eighth year.

And they offered sacrifice according to the law upon the new altar of holocausts which they had made.

According to the time, and according to the day wherein the heathens had defiled it, in the same was it dedicated anew with canticles, and harps, and lutes, and cymbals.

And all the people fell upon their faces, and adored, and blessed up to heaven, him that had prospered them.

And they kept the dedication of altar eight days, and they offered holocausts with joy, and sacrifices of salvation, and of praise.

And they adorned the front of the temple with crowns of gold, and escutcheons, and they renewed the gates, and the chambers, and hanged doors upon them.

And there was exceeding great joy among the people

. . .

And Judas, and his brethren, and all of the church of Israel decreed, that the day of the dedication of the altar should be kept in its season from year to year for eight days, from the five and twentieth day of the month of Casleu, with joy and gladness.

Bible, Old Testament,
apocrypha, I Machabees 4:47–59

NOTES ON SOME OF THE POEMS

AROUND THANKSGIVING is written by Rolfe
Humphries in *Englyn milwr,* a Welsh poetry stanza
of three lines on one rhyme with seven syllables to
each line.

BOOTH KILLED LINCOLN is printed here as it appears in *American Folk Poetry* by Duncan Emrich.
It has been recorded by Mr. Emrich from the singing of Bascom Lamar Lunsford of South Turkey
Creek, North Carolina in a Library of Congress
record. An explanation by Bascom Lunsford tells us
that "the title of this ballad is 'Booth,' or 'Booth
Killed Lincoln.' It's an old fiddle tune, and there
are a few variants of the song. I heard my father
hum it and sing a few of the stanzas when I was just
a boy about six or ten years old."

"But look! a crow comes" by Issa derives its significance
from the traditional Japanese belief that the first
water drawn on New Year's morning is thought to
have magical powers for prolonging life and main-
taining good health. See note on NEW YEAR'S
WATER.

THE CHERRY-TREE CAROL has many versions and many variations and, although it is often associated with Christmas, appears to the editor, in this version, as an Easter ballad. For a symbolic interpretation and further study consult Sandys, *Christmas Carols, Ancient & Modern,* 1833.

COLUMBUS by Alfred, Lord Tennyson has been excerpted in many anthologies. It has much to say about the state and condition of leaders, discoverers, and heroes, and the fickleness of attitudes concerning those who may not, in their own time, be regarded with the respect later accorded them. Perhaps it is even more timely today than when it was written!

"For a fresh start": Issa was the pen name taken by Yatarō Kobayashi, who wrote this poem when he was about twenty-nine years old, about 1792. In *The Year of My Life,* a translation of Issa's Oraga Haru by Nobuyuki Yuasa, the translator informs us that "Issa explains the meaning of this rather unusual pen name in the following manner:

> There is a poet, who, like one possessed, runs east one day and hastens west the next day. He eats breakfast in the province of Kazusa, and seeks a night's lodging in the province of Musashi. He is as helpless as the waves that beat on the shore, and fleeting like the froth that vanishes in a moment. Thus, this poet calls himself "a cup of tea."

THE MASQUE OF QUEENS: Masques were a form of aristocratic entertainment in England during the sixteenth and seventeenth centuries, featuring dance and pantomime at first and later adding dialogue and song. This *Masque of Queens* was celebrated from the House of Fame, by the queen of Great Britain with her ladies at Whitehall on February 2, 1609. It can be found in its entirety in *Ben Jonson: The Complete Masques* edited by Stephen Orgel, Yale University Press, 1969, along with detailed notes by the editor and Jonson's own notes prepared for the 1616 folio.

I am indebted to Professor Steven Bates of the University of California, Los Angeles, for his research and help in locating the complete text of what had been known to me heretofore as brief excerpts under the title "The Witches' Song."

Although full and copious notes are to be found in *The Complete Masques,* a few notes may be of help in reading this excerpt, as follows:

Stephen Orgel explains the words from the 1st, 2nd, 6th, 8th and 9th Hags' speeches as follows: *"quarter"* (a dismembered carcase), *"spurging"* (excretion), *"piper"* (a bagpiper, i.e. lecher), *"got"* (begot), *"church-ale"* (church fair at which ale was sold; the practice was widely condemned), *"Sir Cranion"* (a fly), *"libbard's bane"* (leopard's bane).

NEW YEAR'S WATER: As annotated in *The Gambit Book of Popular Verse,* Geoffrey Grigson takes his text from *Manners & Customs of The People of Tenby,* 1858, thus:

In Tenby and elsewhere in South Wales children went round on New Year's morning with a bunch of evergreens and water drawn from a well, and sprinkled householders and everyone in each house, singing this song. The custom is described in T. M. Owen's *Welsh Folk Customs,* 1968.

levy-dew: (?) the early form levedi or lavedi, for (Our) Lady, or French *lever-Dieu,* Elevation of the Host, so that the third line would celebrate the Bread, the Wine, and the water. *Fair Maid:* (?) Our Lady.

PIETA: Other poems of Jesus Christ and Easter may be found in Rilke's *The Life of the Virgin Mary.*

RESURRECTION: Note the mention here of the Jewish Passover or Pesach, which commemorates the Exodus of the Jews from Egypt and is marked by a Seder dinner, at which the "unleavened bread" (matzos) is eaten, as well as the reference to black slavery with which the poet is chiefly concerned.

THIS CROSSE-TREE HERE: It should be of interest to those who feel that "shape" poems are contemporary to note that Robert Herrick lived from 1591–1674.

TO A YOUNG WRETCH: This poem is undoubtedly more in line with our ecological concerns of today than when it was written.

TO HIS EXCELLENCY GEORGE WASHINGTON: Although the diction and tone of this poem is perhaps alien to many readers of this century, it is included here as typical of the period. Phillis Wheatley was born in Africa, taken as a slave to Boston about 1761, and she later married what was then described as a "free Negro."

TO THE VETERANS OF THE ABRAHAM LINCOLN BRIGADE: The Abraham Lincoln Brigade refers to those Americans who fought for the Spanish Republic against Franco, Mussolini, and Hitler.

UNTO MY VALENTINE: I am indebted to Ann Sanford, editor of *The Women Poets in English* for introducing me to this fifteenth century poem. This letter and poem have been kept by the Paston family over several generations. The letter was written to Margery Brews's future husband, John Paston III, whom she married in 1477—five hundred years ago!

"When Lilacs Last in the Dooryard Bloom'd" is generally considered Whitman's masterpiece. It is excerpted here to introduce the three symbols that influenced the poet at the time. The evening star—

unusually bright in March of 1865, which seemed
to Whitman, in Washington, a portent for the end
of the war—did indeed become obscured when he
returned to Brooklyn between Good Friday and
Easter Sunday and learned of Lincoln's death. Re-
turning to Washington on Easter Monday, he
found the lilacs in full bloom, and it was these
flowers that covered the coffin of Lincoln. Thus,
the star, lilacs, and death combined to produce
this powerful elegy, which should be read in its entirety.

INDEX OF AUTHORS

INDEX OF TITLES

INDEX OF FIRST LINES

INDEX OF TRANSLATORS